In Praise of Anthony J. Cirone's
The Great American Symphony Orchestra

Even for the most avid concertgoer, Tony Cirone's entertaining description of the experience of a professional orchestral musician will provide many valuable insights. Ultimately, Tony's book is an illuminating description of the profound, complex, and rewarding creation of musical performances, told from the perspective of someone who has spent decades both as a musician and an astute observer of others around him.

— Brent Assink — Executive Director, San Francisco Symphony

I am in awe of what musicians do. They are the stars who make the music come alive. I worked with Tony for many of the 14 years that I was President of the San Francisco Symphony and he made my job fun and interesting. There is, and always will be, a tightrope to walk between the needs of the union members and the needs of the institution. Tony bridged this gap when he chaired the Players' Committee. This book is a must read for all people who serve on the boards of America's great orchestras and for all the young musicians who join these orchestras. He has caught the essence, the life, in this unique world of top orchestras. It was a joy to read.

— Nancy Hellman Bechtle — Past President, San Francisco Symphony; Chairman, Presidio Trust; Board Member, Charles Schwab

Orchestral audiences see before them a stage filled with nearly one hundred performers. Most of these musicians spend their entire playing careers contained to their seats in a small space, their view is limited to the music and the conductor. An exception is the standing percussionists at the rear of the orchestra who are uniquely blessed with a far wider field of vision and mobility.

Percussionist Anthony Cirone, after a long and successful performing career with the San Francisco Symphony, shares his own expanded view in a fascinating new book, *The Great American Symphony Orchestra*. He brilliantly takes the audience behind the scenes and describes how the complexity of the orchestra's internal dynamics impact the life-long careers and the artistry of those one hundred awesomely skilled musicians.

> — Keith Brion — Conductor

Anthony Cirone's insight into the professional world of music and passion for this career is matched only by his vast experience and extraordinary talent. This wonderful book, impossible to put down once you start reading it, gives a glimpse of that world few come to know as well as this renowned musician. Each page is filled with stories and anecdotes gleaned from his illustrious career; each word capturing the essence of the wonder that is *The Great American Symphony Orchestra*.

> — Peter Loel Boonshaft — Professor of Music, Hofstra University; Author: *Teaching Music with Passion*; Conductor, Lecturer, and Educator

Tony is dead on: an insider who knows the joys and tensions of working in a symphony orchestra. The pressure of trying to do your best in front of 3000 critics and going home to face the most demanding critic—yourself—is one of the most exhilarating experiences that few are able to obtain.

> — Morris Lang — Musician, New York Philharmonic

This witty, informative book answers every question a reader may have about how major orchestras function, and addresses many other issues inquisitive minds may never have thought of. I recommend it enthusiastically to professionals and the general public alike.

> — Jorge Mester — Conductor Laureate, Aspen Music Festival; Music Director, Louisville Orchestra; Music Director, Naples Philharmonic Orchestra

With this book, Anthony Cirone takes us off the concert stage and leads us backstage to be a part of the behind-the-scenes world of who makes music, with a fascinating look at musicians and conductors, temperaments and personalities, composers and managers, and all the people who make a concert an adventure. *The Great American Symphony Orchestra* is written in such an easy-going manner, it's as if the author were in private conversation with us in our living rooms, conveyed to us in an effortless style, highly informative, and filled with a rich serving of anecdotal asides that will make your next trip to a concert hall a more thoughtful and rewarding experience.

> — William A. Verdone — Patron of the Arts; Secretary, NYC based symphony orchestra, Ensemble212; Member, Berlioz Society

The Great American ★ Symphony Orchestra

A Behind-the-Scenes Look at Its Artistry, Passion, and Heartache

ANTHONY J. CIRONE

Foreword by William Kraft

Published By
MEREDITH MUSIC PUBLICATIONS
a division of G.W. Music, Inc.
4899 Lerch Creek Ct., Galesville, MD 20765
http://meredithmusic.com

MEREDITH MUSIC PUBLICATIONS and its stylized double M logo
are trademarks of
MEREDITH MUSIC PUBLICATIONS, a division of G.W. Music, Inc.

Editor: Josie Cirone
Cover Photo Credit: Chris Wahlberg/San Francisco Symphony
Cover design: Shawn Girsberger

International Standard Book Number: 978-1-57463-174-6
Cataloging-in-Publication Data is on file with the Library of Congress
Library of Congress Control Number: 2011932915
Printed and bound in U.S.A.

DEDICATED

to Josie

The idea for this book came from my wife after I presented a lecture on the profession of orchestral musicians. Besides providing the inspiration for the book, Josie spent countless hours editing the manuscript in order to create a masterful narrative. For all her contributions to my career, I dedicate this book.

ACKNOWLEDGEMENTS

With appreciation to Jerry Gregory, author, historian, and educator for his editorial comments, formatting suggestions, and letters of encouragement.

ය

A special thank you to John Kieser, General Manager of the San Francisco Symphony, for his assistance with details concerning management and operations; Don Carroll (Bass Clarinet) for providing valuable correspondence and insight; Laurie McGaw (Associate Principal Trumpet) and Tom Hemphill (Percussionist) for their contributions regarding the accuracy and content of past events.

ය

Sincere gratitude to my immediate family: Anthony, Liz, Chris, and Mark.

ය

CONTENTS

FOREWORD

"More than you ever wanted to know about the symphony orchestra" is an apt subtitle to Anthony Cirone's vastly informative *The Great American Symphony Orchestra.*

We have a dilemma here. The music performed by a symphony orchestra engages the spiritual and emotional elements of our beings so powerfully that one is reluctant to consider the mundane forces necessary to bring it into reality. On the other hand, the institution of the symphony orchestra is such a majestic enterprise that one may well be curious to know how it all comes about. There are so many questions an avid listener would like to have answered:

- How does a musician gain a position in an orchestra?
- What is the relationship between the orchestra and the board of directors?
- How is the board constituted?
- How does the orchestra travel on tours?
- How do the players get along with each other?
- How is the repertory determined?
- And the great question for both orchestra and its supporters: How does it survive financially—a really BIG problem.

All of these questions are discussed in *The Great American Symphony Orchestra* but there is so much more that is covered: from the arcane to the mundane, the serious to the humorous, and from the historical to the anecdotal.

One learns not only about the symphony orchestra as an institution, but also about the everyday lives of the musicians and their backgrounds. Cirone is an excellent musician who reveals himself as a gifted writer. The writing is notable by its clarity, conciseness and knowledge. There are moments of delicious humor, much of which reveals the inner personality of the orchestra.

The Great American Symphony Orchestra is aptly titled. Major American orchestras are on par with the much older and more established orchestras of Europe. This book should be available, not only in bookstores everywhere, but also in the lobbies and museum shops of the auditoriums where orchestras perform. I say "Bravo" to Tony Cirone for such a wonderful and valuable contribution to the literature of the world of music.

—William Kraft

Mr. Kraft has received numerous commissions and prizes as a composer, including two Kennedy Center Friedheim Awards; two Guggenheim Fellowships; two Ford Foundation commissions; fellowships from the Huntington Hartford Foundation and the National Endowment for the Arts; the American Academy and Institute of Arts and Letters Music Award.

PREFACE

I still remember the first time I attended a concert at Carnegie Hall and the emotions that stirred within me as I anticipated what was about to take place in this magnificently-adorned auditorium. I was taken aback by its immense size and fascinated by the way my voice rebounded off the interior walls that had been designed to transform, absorb, and embrace the nature of sound.

In preparation for the evening's performance, a member of the stage crew adjusted chairs as the librarian placed music folders on each player's stand. Musicians wandered in and located their seats among the hundred or so that had been carefully arranged in a methodically-designed semicircle. I watched the clarinetist assemble his instrument, wiping each part, inside and out, with a soft cloth—fitting the sections together with the precision of a surgeon's hand. Moistening the reed of the mouthpiece, he attached it to the body of the clarinet and the first musical vibrations of the evening resonated throughout the hall. One by one, other musicians joined in, at first with a simple note or two, and before long scales and arpeggios could be heard as more players entered the stage. Eventually, the entire orchestra warmed up, tuning or practicing difficult passages—the result, a cacophony of sound, resplendent in all its dissonance.

The onstage lights brightened as the room grew dim, sounds from the orchestra and audience faded away and silence filled the space. The concertmaster entered to polite applause and with a nod of his head to the principal oboist, the sonorous tone of **A** was sounded. Violinists, violists, cellists, and bassists tuned to that exact vibration and then adjusted the remaining strings of their instruments. The oboist gave another **A** to the brass and woodwinds who also tuned to the same pitch. After a few seconds of complete silence the conductor emerged—this time, to resounding applause. Taking a bow, mounting the podium, and raising the baton, the performance began.

Patrons of the arts cannot fully realize the copious amount of detailed preparation that occurs before such a moment as this can transpire. Some musicians take as many as fifty auditions before being selected as tenured members of a major symphony orchestra. Years of devoted practice, study, and experience are necessary in order to reach the level of excellence required to perform with such an organization. Each performer is chosen for his or her distinct characteristics which, when blended together with other artists, are heard as one voice, creating the inspired sounds of symphonic music.

This book is intended to provide music lovers with an in-depth look at life in a symphony orchestra, including its relationship with management and staff who run the day-to-day operations. I, therefore, invite those who usually enter a concert hall through the front doors, to meet me at the stage entrance and take a behind-the-scenes tour of *The Great American Symphony Orchestra*.

AJC

THE MUSICAL FAMILY

Who is there that, in logical words, can express the effect music has on us? A kind of inarticulate, unfathomable speech, which leads us to the edge of the infinite and lets us for moments gaze into that!

—Thomas Carlyle 1795- Sat 1851

Try to imagine an extended family with more than one hundred people (parents, grandparents, aunts, uncles, cousins, and siblings); then, think of them all gathered at a family reunion. This is a glimpse of what it's like to be part of a symphony orchestra. An orchestra is not very different from other families—they socialize, marry, divorce, become ill, move, change jobs, and die. New members join this organization through the audition process and others visit for a time as substitute players. Orchestras also have a "patriarch" or a "matriarch," called the Music Director, who lords over the orchestra family as its head and conducts many of the concerts. All conductors interpret the elements of a musical score (tempo, dynamics, phrasing, and character), but a music director's responsibilities also encompass the orchestra's artistic standards, personnel, tours, recordings, including repertoire and soloists, during the weeks he or she conducts. In fact, it's been said that a conductor functions as one of the last remaining dictators within a working community—more to say about this later!

The performing component of a musical family consists of approximately one hundred musicians, the size of a small business—yet, any similarities to other enterprises end there. Most office employees have the flexibility of arriving early, leaving late, and taking breaks as needed since much of their work is done on an independent basis. An orchestra is different in this respect because all one hundred (plus) members must be present before the business of making music can take place. No one player can show up late or leave early in this profession. When a brass, woodwind, or percussion player is absent, the part is not able to be covered by anyone else since these musicians are one-on-a-part players and the score cannot be properly rehearsed. If a performer calls in sick, a substitute player must be hired to fill that chair. It's like a line of falling dominoes, when one is taken out, the entire sequence comes to a halt.

Businessmen and women work in offices or cubicles but with a symphony orchestra, performers sit together onstage without the use of partitions. In fact, two string players share one music stand. The personal-relationship dynamic is, therefore, exponentially increased because of this close proximity. It is also possible for an orchestra member to sit next to the same person throughout his or her entire career (which often can cause heartaches) since there is no mechanism in place to transfer to a different chair (except for demotion or audition for an open position).

Charles Blackman elaborates on the nature of a symphony orchestra in *Behind the Baton* (Charos Enterprises, Inc., NY):

A modern symphony orchestra, in itself, is an awe-inspiring medium. It is seen as a group of people who have acquired an ability to read the musical notation and play upon certain readily available instruments—routinely expected to be present and perform on cue as though, together, they made up a mechanical device. In actual fact, there is a great deal more to an orchestra than meets the eye. Deriving from the culture of many civilizations, it is the most responsive, the most satisfying, and above all, the most forgiving instrument one can have.

When a conductor begins a rehearsal, all musicians must be seated, in tune, and ready to perform at the identical rate of speed as every other player. Similar to precision engineering, no discernable tolerances in rhythm can be allowed when executing music notation at such a high level of accuracy. In the business world, it's possible for individual components to be manufactured in different buildings or countries before being assembled for sale. Musical scores, however, are performed at the same moment, by the same people, and in the same place.

The ratio of management (administration) to orchestra musicians is also significantly greater (one-to-one) than that found in industry. In other words, it takes the same amount of management and staff (one hundred) to administer the day-to-day operations of a major symphony orchestra.

The following excerpt, depicting the relationship between a music director and a board of directors, is taken from an interview by Helen M. Thompson (former Executive of the League of American Orchestras) with Max Rudolf (former Music Director of the Cincinnati Symphony Orchestra) in *The American Symphony Orchestra* by Henry Swoboda *(Basic Books, Inc., NY)*:

> *My Board has never told me what I should or should not play. We have discussed certain reactions on the part of subscribers and newspapers, but they do not exert the slightest degree of pressure. It might interest you to learn that a gentlemen's agreement exists between the Board and myself. When I was engaged, the President of the Board told me: "We think that you should have full freedom in all artistic matters within the possibilities of our budget. We will never interfere. You can play what you want, you can engage musicians as you see fit, as well as soloists, and so forth, because," he added, "we think that is the only way you can be successful. If you are not successful, we are sure you would not want to stay."*

Nancy Bechtle, Past President of the San Francisco Symphony for fourteen years, shares her ideas regarding the relationship between a Music Director and the Board of Directors:

> *In many of the big orchestras, the Board President or Chairman is the CEO of the organization. It would be awkward for the music director to report to the executive director or vice versa. They both, therefore, report to the Board. Actually, the biggest responsibility for the Board is the hiring of both the Music Director and the Executive Director. The musical vision of the orchestra is mainly the responsibility of the Music Director but there are so many financial implications of those decisions that there must be some oversight from Board and Management.*

As a member of the San Francisco Symphony, I have also observed the relationship between a music director, an executive director, and the board of directors. The music director is responsible for all artistic matters for this non-profit corporation. The executive director is in charge of management and oversees fundraising in support of the orchestra budget (upwards of $100 million for major American symphony orchestras). The board of directors' main responsibility is to hire the executive director and music director.

The greatest problem orchestras face today is an inability to raise funds to meet the yearly budget. Since ticket sales are only a small percentage of the income necessary to maintain a symphony orchestra, a large number of administrative staff are hired to solicit gifts and donations from individuals to corporate donors. A great deal of this fund-raising activity is for the Endowment Fund that provides a steady income for the General Fund (Appendix B: Symphony Administration & Staff Positions, Page 201, Development).

The recent stock market decline has had a tremendous impact on orchestras since they depend on a certain percentage of investment growth for income. A major symphony orchestra has the ability to withstand a temporary financial crisis, but middle-level orchestras do not fare as well, with many of them going out of business or reorganizing as part-time, player-managed organizations, performing only five to ten series of concerts a year.

Another source of symphony revenue comes from volunteer organizations that raise funds from a variety of sources: a resale shop, symphony store, special concerts, and volunteer councils that operate within the local community. One of the more popular fund-raising events in San Francisco is the *Black and White Ball* (the party of the year) with its evening of music, food, and dancing. Several city blocks are utilized for this gala event, including Davies Hall, the War Memorial Opera House, City Hall, and a variety of other venues, including tents that are set up to host musical groups, ranging from the classic sound of the Symphony to Heavy Metal bands.

An orchestra is divided into four major sections: woodwinds, brass, percussion, and strings. This order follows the same sequence listed on musical scores (Appendix A: Instruments as Listed in a Musical Score, Page 199).

Woodwind and brass sections have a Principal First Chair, Associate Principal Chair, Second and Third Chairs, each one commanding a different salary. For instance, the third chair clarinetist plays the Eb parts and is on a higher pay scale than the second chair clarinetist (usually, the higher the chair, the higher the salary).

The Percussion Section has a Principal Timpanist, a Principal Percussionist, and three additional Percussionists. This section is not as structured as others and although these musicians are able to play all percussion instruments, orchestras vary as to the division of parts. Some sections are set up so players perform in only one of the four main categories for standard classical repertoire, that is, bass drum, cymbals, snare drum, or keyboard percussion (xylophone, orchestra bells, marimba, and vibraphone), whereas other orchestras rotate players among these four areas. A compelling reason *not* to rotate percussionists is to give them an opportunity to perfect their interpretation on the same instrument since classical repertoire is repeated over the years.

Two string players share one music stand, however, in other sections, every performer has an individual stand. The inside string player (who sits away from the audience) is the page turner. The outside musician continues to perform while the inside player briefly stops to turn the page. String sections, except for titled positions (Associate and Assistant Principals), rotate chairs on a regular basis. In the past, string players sat with the same stand partner for most of their careers. It's different today, these players now sit next to different musicians on a weekly basis. The concertmaster, specifically appointed by the music director, is generally the highest-paid member of an orchestra.

As part of this extended family, it's important to consider the librarians. Every symphony orchestra has a Principal Librarian and at least one Assistant Librarian. These men and women are an integral component of the musical family since they allow it to operate in a smooth and efficient manner by preparing scores and parts for all rehearsals and performances. Orchestra librarians insert bowings for string players, add or delete sections of music requested by conductors, erase pencil markings added by previous players, consult with conductors regarding score preparation, and proof read new music. The San Francisco Symphony's Principal Librarian, John Van Winkle, summarizes the most important part of his job: *For me, it is having the right music, in the right place, at the right time, properly prepared.*

Librarians place orchestra parts on music stands before each session. This staff also maintains a large selection of scores and parts for hundreds of compositions, study scores, and reference material for research. Musicians can check out music weeks in advance of a first rehearsal to learn new music or to practice difficult excerpts. A copy machine is an indispensible tool for the library staff because some players require parts in larger print or to be reassembled for page turns. Librarians must be familiar with music publishers throughout the world in order to locate composers' scores and editions for purchase, rental, or replacement.

All orchestras have a Stage Manager and Crew who are responsible for the onstage placement of stands, chairs, the podium, sound shields (on the backs of chairs or between sections), piano, organ, large percussion instruments (bass drum, tam-tam, chimes, timpani, and xylophone), special chairs or stools for certain players, and other unusual equipment as needed. This crew provides storage facilities, maintenance of equipment, instrument cases for traveling, construction and placement of risers, canopies for outdoor events, and acoustical retrofits. The stage manager is also in charge of all technical aspects of sound, lighting, and recording.

The stage crew arrives two hours before a rehearsal or performance to set up and remain until the end of a session to make adjustments or changes for the next service. When there is a run-out concert (out of the local area with no overnight stay), the crew travels to the new venue hours before the show to unload equipment and to prepare for the performance. At the end of the evening, they reload the truck and return everything to the "home" concert hall. These men (and sometimes women) are an important part of the orchestra family. Musicians depend on them to make sure their chairs, stools, stands, and equipment are placed in the proper position. No section is more dependent on the stage crew than percussionists since their setup is different for every performance. Sometimes, such a large battery of percussion instruments are required (especially for contemporary music) that some of them have to be removed from the stage (between compositions) so others can be added for the next programmed work.

An unusual event happened several years ago during an evening performance of the San Francisco Symphony that involved the stage crew. The program included an overture, a piano concerto, an intermission, and a symphony. At the end of the first piece, the crew rolled the piano onstage for the concerto but before they were halfway across, the front leg collapsed and the piano came crashing down to the floor! The audience was aghast and orchestra members stared in silent amazement. The two crew members froze in place, not believing what had happened. Finally, realizing the piano would not be in working condition, they lifted the front end and rolled it backstage. A few orchestra members came forward to help. Since a representative from management is always present at all performances, he announced that a change in program order would take place. The symphony was to be performed next with the concerto to take place after intermission (with a new piano). When the crew successfully rolled out the second piano, they were given a round of applause from both the audience and orchestra members.

During my thirty-six year career with the San Francisco Symphony, I have worked with a number of stage crews and I particularly remember one group that had the attitude all musicians were complainers, referring to them as *prima donnas*. The percussion section had a particular problem with them. A timpanist uses four "kettle drums" that need to be set up in a particular order. (Timpanists trained in the American system place the largest drum to the player's left; those trained in the European style, place it to the right.) This crew constantly arranged the timpani in the wrong order which affected the section's attitude towards these men. When a new executive director was appointed, one of the first changes he made was to fire the stage manager and crew—not simply because of the timpani incident, but for many other contentious issues.

Musicians have a tremendous amount of responsibility when it comes to performing and when a stage crew cannot carry out their job in a proficient manner, it creates additional stress for everyone. I must say that the most recent Symphony crews have been very professional. In fact, it has become a tradition for the percussion section to take them out to lunch on a yearly basis as a token of our appreciation for their hard work.

An orchestra family also includes a Board of Directors who are responsible for the financial oversight of the organization. These true patrons of the arts provide leadership in the areas of artistic matters and development. Administrators and staff personnel are equally important. Besides managing employees, schedules, guest conductors, soloists, tours, recordings (the list is endless), a great amount of their time is directly related to coordinating fund-raising activities. A typical list of staff descriptions can be found in Appendix B: Symphony Administration & Staff Positions, Page 201.

There are also countless volunteers who host parties, galas, and fund-raising events. Their efforts raise revenue for guest conductors, soloists, musical commissions, the pension fund, tours, recordings, special (free) public concerts, and sabbaticals for orchestra members. The San Francisco Symphony has a Volunteer Council managed by a five-member Executive Board that consists of ten League Presidents who administer volunteer activities throughout the Bay Area (each committee has its own chairperson and staff representatives). The Volunteer Council oversees: The Opening Gala, All San Francisco Concert, Deck the Hall Concert, Black and White Ball, Chinese New Year Celebration, Youth Orchestra Liaison, Recruitment and Placement of Youth Orchestra members, Concerts for Kids, Office Volunteers, Open Rehearsals, Special Events Staffing/Host Committee, Repeat Performance (resale store), the Symphony Store (Davies Hall lobby), and the creation of posters for advertising events.

Orchestra members, no matter what chair or position they hold, do not have the right to criticize or correct a colleague. Although musicians often discuss parts or make suggestions, when it comes to sound, embouchure, fingering, choice of instruments, bows, mallets, or mouthpieces, these decisions are the sole discretion of individual players. Although music directors can address these issues, they are not always well received.

The concertmaster (first chair violin) decides how the first violin section will bow the music before the initial rehearsal (whether to use an up or down bow stroke). First chairs for the second violin, viola, cello, and bass also decide how players in their respective sections bow the music so as to ensure consistent phrasing, dynamics, rhythm, and appearance. This may seem like a straight-forward responsibility but it is not that simple. Jeremy Constant, Assistant Concertmaster of the San Francisco Symphony, Concertmaster of the Marin Symphony and Sun Valley Summer Symphony, contributes this behind-the-scenes look at how this process works:

There are several ways bowings are established before the first rehearsal. With a brand new composition, the concertmaster starts from nothing. In this case, guidance is needed on tempo and, hopefully, metronome markings have been provided by the composer. If something is ambiguous, access to the conductor and/or composer will be necessary before the bowings can be completed. If not, an educated guess must be made using the most flexible bowings. Once the concertmaster has bowed the first violin part, it is distributed to other string principals to collaborate with bowings for their section. If there are complications, they work together to find a good solution.

If the parts are from an orchestra library or a music rental company, they will contain existing bowings. The concertmaster will then use recollections from past performances and knowledge of the conductor's preferences to make appropriate changes. It's important for the library, concertmaster, and conductor to work from the same edition since there are significant differences in phrasing, articulations, and slurs from edition to edition.

Furthermore, there are stylistic differences among conductors within the same piece and bowings that work in one tempo will not work in another. Particularly in Baroque music, the differences in ornamentation, phrasing, and slurring are enormous with different editions and conductors. There also can be very different interpretations within the same edition and previously performed parts may have to be completely altered to meet the conductor's preference.

During rehearsals, the judgment of the concertmaster becomes very important. Depending on the conductor, he or she may not want the rehearsal interrupted to hone a bowing to produce the desired result—even if it's obvious that the printed bowing is an obstacle. Others welcome the immediate positive change when a different bowing would completely transform what the conductor hears into what is desired. There are very few conductors who completely understand that some ensemble problems can be instantly fixed by better bowing choices and uniformity in bowing from section to section.

Discernment regarding how many bowing changes are practical during a rehearsal also has to do with the fact that string sections can become quickly fatigued if there are too many adjustments. To change a bowing, it has to be passed from the front to the back, stand by stand. This takes rehearsal time. The conductor might also make additional verbal requests while musicians are trying to erase an old bowing and correctly write in a new one; so, it's easy to feel things are coming at them too fast. The better the initial bowings work, the less time is spent during rehearsals trying to either fix or work around them.

Another responsibility of the concertmaster, that most non-musicians do not realize, is to decide whether or not the orchestra stands or sits during the applause. When a concert ends, the conductor turns towards the audience to take a bow and then leaves the stage. When the maestro (a title of respect) returns, he or she may ask the concertmaster to stand (along with the entire orchestra) and acknowledge the applause. In this case, the orchestra will be standing when the conductor leaves the stage for the second time. At this point, the concertmaster has the option to continue to stand or to sit down. Musicians follow the concertmaster's lead. If the orchestra is sitting when the conductor returns, he or she receives a solo bow. If the orchestra is standing they, once again, are included in the applause. The decision to give a conductor a solo bow is, therefore, based on the concertmaster's discretion to sit or stand. If the concertmaster and conductor do not get along well, this can be a controversial issue since the orchestra has no say as to whether or not the conductor receives a solo bow. Although this was a problem in the past with the San Francisco Symphony, it has not been a concern in recent history.

Another tradition, no longer practiced in San Francisco, was for the trumpet section to honor a conductor or soloist by playing a *Tusch* (short flourish or fanfare).

Again, this was done at the sole discretion of the trumpet section and became a source of disagreement among orchestra members since no vote was taken as to whether or not a *Tusch* should be played. And, even if a vote were to be taken, it would not have been unanimous—the tradition, therefore, has disappeared.

Musicians often form close friendships with members of their own section. The obvious reason is that these players perform together for most of their careers. An orchestra is given a 15

to 25-minute break (depending on the length of a rehearsal) and where a player assembles backstage also fosters close relationships. For instance, in most orchestras the first and second violins, harp, piano, woodwinds, and percussionists (who sit right of center stage) exit stage right. Violas, cellos, basses, and brass exit stage left. String and woodwind players usually congregate near shelves where their instrument cases are located. Percussionists have a storage room for large instruments and trunks—consequently, they hang out there. Some orchestra members use the locker room or orchestra lounge for breaks. The point is that members of an orchestra tend to associate with musicians offstage because of where they take their breaks.

Carpooling also encourages lifetime friendships. For most of my career, I carpooled with two violinists and we have remained very close friends. Carpools are a welcome bonus to an otherwise monotonous commute (two services a day—one in the morning and another in the evening—two or three days a week). For awhile we had five musicians in our group. One person drove a Volkswagen Beetle and we were quite a sight to behold, exiting this vehicle with not only five players but two violins, a viola, and cello.

John Wyre, former Timpanist of the Toronto Symphony Orchestra and an extra (substitute) player with the Boston Symphony, addressed the intimate relationships that develop within an orchestra. Not only was John a talented timpanist and percussionist, but the founder of NEXUS, a world-famous percussion ensemble. John expressed immense spiritual insight regarding the depth of relationships between musicians in *Touched by Sound* (Buka Music, Canada):

Music teaches us that the preciousness of family lies in the fact that we are centered and strengthened by our relatedness. The attraction and the balance of opposites in the ebb and flow of relationships challenge us and lead to growth. We must balance the individual's freedom to flower with the responsibility of the parts to the whole.

Reasonableness comes from knowing that we are all in this together. Individuality equals unique perceptions and unique understanding, and so we inspire and challenge each other. Moderation, working in harmony with our life lessons, is essential in navigating the ancient pathways of responsibility and reasonableness.

Composers, performers, conductors, and audiences all have unique perceptions and individual ideas about every aspect of music. Melody, Line, Color, Harmony, Pulse, all conjure up images from our unique perspectives. Music reconciles differences and offers us the possibility of unification.

A former colleague, Walter Green (Principal Bassoon), also recognized the interactions that exist among symphony musicians in *Golden Tones—Memoirs of a Musician's Life* (Pacific Transcriptions, Mendocino, CA):

You build camaraderie over the years in an orchestra. There's nothing like it. The camaraderie is there between men and women all the way all the time. This wonderful fellowship that develops between the musicians makes an orchestra better, because playing with someone and having a very good ensemble is so important. That's a huge part of it. And you can't depend on the conductor for everything. It's not possible.

Although members of a family have hobbies, this is not always the case with symphony artists, many of whom have no interests outside of music. Some orchestra members hold professorships at universities or teach privately; others play chamber music, publish method books, and a few are serious composers and conductors. While these endeavors are admirable, they all relate to music. The fact is, to excel in any one area takes a great amount of energy and when family obligations are added into the mix, little time is left for anything else in a busy musician's schedule.

For some, the demands of a full-time symphony career are rewarding enough without pursuing any other activities. I know a number of orchestra members who dread the thought of retiring for fear they will not know what to do without an orchestra routine. Yet, there are those who, besides being active in extracurricular musical avocations, have a passion for hobbies. Some performers are joggers, bikers, hikers, golfers, car and boat enthusiasts, and others enjoy cooking, wine making, and brewing beer. One San Francisco Symphony player mastered the ancient Japanese board game, *Go*. Two performers are accomplished magicians who entertained colleagues during intermissions and tours. There are also the entrepreneurs who own businesses, and one player is a graphic artist. Although there are many talented wood workers in the orchestra, none have risen to the level of Principal Percussionist, Jack Van Geem, who is currently building a 4200 square foot home—by himself—in Mendocino, California. But, if this was a contest for the most unusual hobby, my vote would go to Jeremy Constant, Assistant Concertmaster, who took seven years and three months to complete the construction of a Vans Aircraft, model RV7A, single-engine, two-seat, aerobatic aircraft with cruise speeds of up to 200 mph. As for me, I have been an organic gardener since 1970 (before it was fashionable) and still continue to grow my own vegetables.

An orchestra rehearses about ten hours a week with an additional ten hours devoted to performances. This does not include the necessary preparation required to learn parts, maintain technique, and to warm up before all sessions. It is not uncommon to have extra rehearsals and, occasionally, five performances in one week instead of the usual four. There are run-out concerts within the local community that also add travel time to a performer's schedule. National and international tours require musicians to be on the road for another four to six weeks a year. As is evident, orchestra members spend quite a bit of time with coworkers and, as with most extended families, some players do not get along well with one another—which can lead to heartaches. I have a friend in another orchestra who has not spoken to a member of his section for over thirty-five years! It's also not uncommon for musicians to marry within an orchestra but it's rare to find a married couple who both win auditions in the same orchestra.

An orchestral working environment is unusual, to say the least, and is especially challenging when there are offstage disagreements. But, whatever happens behind the scenes, does not affect a musician's performance onstage. There is little time to reflect upon personal issues while playing because so much concentration is needed to perform the thousands of notes in any given composition. Orchestra members are highly-trained professionals who devote themselves to perfecting their musical skills.

Performance-related injuries are a serious problem in this business. String players, more than any other musicians, are afflicted with adverse physical conditions because of the repetitive movements of their bowing arm (right) and the way the left arm must be held to support the violin or viola so their fingers can fly over the fingerboard with dexterity. In addition to raising both arms for extended periods of time, string players must also tilt their head so the chin can support the instrument. Try doing this for two hours and you will probably need a chiropractic adjustment! When these artists have a few measures of rest, they occasionally lower their right bowing arm to allow blood to flow back into it. But, when the left arm is lowered, all that remains to support the instrument is the chin. Because there are so many injuries in this profession, management now subsidizes weekly *Feldenkrais* (body-movement awareness) classes which are mainly attended by string players. According to John Kieser, General Manager of the San Francisco Symphony, since these classes were initiated, there have been fewer worker-compensation claims.

Such a close working environment can create problematic situations in this musical family, and when they occur, musicians are advised to bring them to the Personnel Manager. This person is a very important member of the musical family because he or she is a direct liaison between the orchestra and management and is responsible for enforcing all areas of the contract. Many complaints revolve around noise levels, the use of cologne and/or perfume, placement of music stands, uncomfortable chairs, lighting, and so forth. Decibel levels are of particular concern (primarily produced by the brass, percussion, and piccolo). The musical symbol for loud is *f*, but I have seen as many as six *fortes* in a part (*ffffff*), the equivalent of very, very, very, very, very, very, loud. What can a performer do when a composer indicates such a dynamic? It's not the musician's fault when he or she is asked to perform at such deafening levels—the problem lies with the composer. Of course, it is not possible to address this issue with most of them since they usually do not attend rehearsals and many are dead!

Noise levels vary greatly, depending on repertoire. The Occupational Safety & Health Administration (OSHA), a federal agency that monitors decibel levels in the workplace, requires management to provide orchestra members with ear plugs for all sessions. Although some players find them uncomfortable and refuse to wear these noise-reducing devices, they have certainly made a difference (in addition to the plastic shields used as buffers in front of the brass and percussion sections). Shields can also be attached to the backs of individual chairs and any player can request one. When a percussionist has to produce a loud noise, for example, a gun or cannon shot, the player might be asked to test the decibel level during a rehearsal to get approval from orchestra members. Before ear plugs were available, musicians suffered from loud decibel levels but their complaints fell on deaf ears (no pun intended). A second violin player who sat directly in front of the suspended cymbal devised an interesting solution to protect his hearing. He placed the eraser end of a pencil into his ear (pencil attached) which was quite a comical sight to behold.

When there are moments of very loud music and a musician decides not to use ear plugs, he or she may employ the best sound-reducing technique ever devised—a finger in each ear. This, of course, only works if the person is not playing at the time! The next time you are at a concert that demands loud music, notice if any players are using this age-old technique. At one point, the music director of the San Francisco Symphony moved the harp player to a spot in front of the suspended cymbal. This player now sits with his fingers in his ears when cymbal crashes become overwhelming. During rehearsals, when a particularly loud entrance approached, I tapped his shoulder to warn him that a crash was about to take place. Needless to say, we have remained friends.

As a percussionist, I sat on a stool towards the back of the stage. From this position, I could easily observe all members of the orchestra family. To my left, I had a clear view of the timpani, trumpet, trombone, tuba, and French horn sections. Far left, I saw the entire bass section. The woodwinds were in front of me (to the left), so I looked at the backs of their heads. Although the violas were at an angle, I had full view of the cellos. The second violins and first violins (in that order) were directly in front of me with the harp and piano close by. Since most classical repertoire has a limited amount of percussion, I had hours to contemplate the workings of an orchestra. Brahms Symphony No. 4, for example, only calls for the use of one percussionist who plays triangle in the third movement. Dvořák's *New World Symphony* also uses just one player for both the triangle and cymbal in the *Scherzo*. The most unusual example of limited percussion is Bruckner's Symphony No. 7, with only a single cymbal crash and a triangle roll (performed by two players) during the *Adagio* of this ninety-minute work. These composers, therefore, have left me with a lot of time to observe the *modus operandi* of an orchestra.

Until the San Francisco Symphony moved to Davies Hall in 1980, the orchestra performed in the War Memorial Opera House that did not have seating behind the stage. The new hall now gave ticket holders a different perspective of the orchestra since they could look directly down on musicians while they performed and see the conductor face-on. During previous years in the Opera House, some woodwind and brass players were able to conceal reading material or do crossword puzzles during *tacet* movements which was no longer possible in the newly-designed Davies Hall. There were also musicians who had the uncanny ability to take short naps during long periods of rests, and although the audience, management, and other performers may not have noticed, it did not get past my roving eyes!

From my strategic position I was able to observe how some orchestra members "moved" while performing, which not only helps to create a musical phrase and assists in controlling dynamics, but also allows the audience to perceive a player's artistry and sense the energy and passion of the music. Within the string sections (where all musicians play the same part), it was interesting to note how different performers embraced the use of body movement, some swaying quite passionately, while others were less animated, hardly stirring at all.

I guess it's fair to say the musical family is like any other family with its passion and heartache—they laugh, cry, rejoice, grieve, support, comfort, disagree, fight, and reconcile. But as performers, whatever problems occur offstage stay there because onstage, we are one amazing FAMILY!

HOW DO I GET TO CARNEGIE HALL?

The notes I handle no better than many pianists. But the
pauses between the notes—ah, that is where the art resides!

—Artur Schnabel

Practice, practice, practice is the correct answer to the question: *How do I get to Carnegie Hall?* Professional musicians practice constantly; in fact, they become slaves to their instruments. Even as young children, these artists-to-be spent years developing technique and preparing etudes for lessons—time that often replaced social activities. Today, youngsters are expected to excel in academics, participate in religious activities, sports, and community projects, leaving them with little opportunities for other pursuits. So, how do serious music students find those extra hours in the day to practice? The sad answer is by curtailing social interactions with friends and family.

Toby Perlman, wife of the famous violinist, Itzhak Perlman, directs a summer music program for young, gifted string players. Besides a vigorous curriculum of lessons and performances, the school also nurtures these developing artists in a supportive environment. The inclusion of social skills for these musicians, who spend most of their early years in the solitude of a practice room, caught my attention. The following quote is taken from the school's website *(www.perlmanmusicprogram.org)*:

> *Boasting a remarkable student to faculty ratio of better than 2:1, the faculty, led by Itzhak Perlman, includes some of the most highly respected and sought-after pedagogues in the world. This helps create an environment that provides the valuable resources necessary to nurture remarkable talent, while at the same time promoting both leadership and real life social skills.*

Very few occupations demand the discipline, training, and education as that of professional musicians, most of whom began to prepare for such a career very early in life. In fact, I started to take music lessons at seven years of age and from that day forward I always studied with a music teacher. Although some instruments are more difficult to master than others, all performers spend countless hours and years of relentless practice developing the techniques necessary to compete on a professional level. This preparation can be compared to training for the Olympics. Since the competition for a position in a major symphony orchestra is so overwhelming, it's important for parents to pay particular attention to children who show an aptitude and a desire in this field. Music students at the university level easily "burn out" because of the additional hours demanded of them for practice and performances. That's why, when freshmen enter my studio for the first time, I tell them to remember two things: *Eat and Sleep!*

Budding musicians who have made the decision to dedicate themselves to mastering an instrument can sharpen their skills as symphony players by joining youth orchestras. Since most elementary schools no longer offer the option to perform in an orchestra, privately-run youth orchestras have become very successful. The San Francisco Symphony Youth Orchestra, with its extraordinary artistic and financial resources, is a "jewel" in the Bay Area. Students who qualify for acceptance are provided with coaching from members of the Symphony and receive training from conductors of merit, including the music director.

Novelist Flannery O'Connor describes the dedication required in her profession as a writer:

> *Every morning between nine and twelve I go to my room and sit before a piece of paper. Many times, I just sit for three hours with no ideas coming to me. But, I know one thing: If an idea does come to me between nine and twelve, I am there ready for it.*

Musicians cannot simply sit and wait for inspiration— they must go the extra mile and actually practice. The dedication expressed by O'Connor, in addition to a love of music and a yearning to excel, are crucial ingredients for those wanting to pursue a career as a professional performer.

Playing a musical instrument requires great finger dexterity or hand and arm control. Wind players also have to develop proper embouchure (adjustment of the mouth to the mouthpiece, involving the lips, facial, and jaw muscles) in order to produce a proper tone. My touring roommate played the trumpet and constantly "buzzed" the mouthpiece to maintain his embouchure. But, in my opinion, the most difficult instruments to master are the strings (violin, viola, cello, and bass), French horn, oboe, and bassoon (double reeds).

Paul Salmon and Robert Meyer elaborate on the difficulties that face those who hope to find employment in a musical career in *Notes from the Green Room* (Lexington Books, NY):

> *Musical skills exceed many other skills in terms of complexity, potential level of refinement, capacity for expressiveness, and preparatory rigor. It is well known that relatively few performing musicians rise to prominent levels of professional accomplishment, so arduous and demanding is the pathway leading to this plateau. Becoming a performer is not for the faint of heart. Not only does one have to persist through years of rigorous training, but the intense competition any young performer must face is sufficient to discourage all but the persistent few.*
>
> *Many musicians, possessed of marvelous skills and highly-attuned musical sensitivities, flounder during their training for any of a variety of reasons. Some become discouraged by the sheer amount of work, in return for which only the most tenuous promise of subsequent reward is offered. Some, because of practice regiments that leave little time to eat or sleep, experience burn out or incur physical*

injuries during their formative years of development. Still others fall victim to psychological vulnerabilities associated with performing, chief among these being prolonged stress and anxiety that can markedly detract from the expressive capabilities of even the most skilled performer.

Another impediment that can hinder a musician from pursuing a career as an orchestral performer is a lack of "team spirit." It makes no difference whether a person works in a corporate environment with its bureaucratic system of presidents, vice-presidents, and managers or a musician who performs under the baton of a conductor, team spirit is an essential quality if one is to survive professionally and emotionally. The ability to follow directions is another important attribute but, for musicians, it's critical. Some performers may not like a particular conductor's interpretation of a musical score, nevertheless, it is the player's responsibility to perform the music according to the conductor's interpretation. There's a saying in music circles: "A symphony orchestra is made up of one hundred conductors." In other words, all musicians have an opinion as to how fast, slow, loud, soft, *legato* or *staccato* (slurred or separated) any given phrase should sound, but it is the conductor's prerogative to interpret the score and the player's responsibility to perform it according to his or her wishes.

Musicians who have difficulty changing, adjusting, correcting, or refining a passage, on the spot, will have trouble functioning as members of an orchestra. It is also important to note that when a conductor addresses a player during a rehearsal, no discussion should follow since it's not the time to have a conversation or question these remarks. The correct response should be a simple, "Yes, Maestro!" For instance, if a musician is asked to play softer, it's not appropriate for the player to discuss the dynamic listed in the part. The proper answer, again, should be, "Yes, Maestro!" If the orchestra member wants to address the request, he or she can meet with the conductor during a break or after a rehearsal. A performer will never win an onstage argument with a conductor.

Percussionists sometimes find themselves in a quandary when a conductor makes a remark, such as: "The snare drum is too loud, use softer sticks." When such a statement is made, it is obvious the maestro is not familiar with the use of percussion equipment because a snare drum is played with wooden sticks. Any other type of mallets, such as brushes or felt-tip sticks, must be specifically requested by a composer because, although they may sound softer, the entire sound of the drum is changed when they are used. Instead of holding an onstage conversation with the conductor regarding the proper way to play a snare drum, the player should simply take the sticks in question and pretend to exchange them for a different pair. Then, using the same sticks, just play softer! It would be more appropriate for conductors to express the changes they want to hear (in this case, to play softer) than to tell the musician how to achieve the result (unless they are well versed in the use of the instrument). Very few conductors have detailed knowledge of the workings of a percussion section.

The *Nutcracker Suite* by Tchaikovsky is one of the most frequently performed compositions in the literature. During one section of music, the tambourine has very soft repeated rhythms of quick thirty-second notes. I play this part in my usual fashion by placing the instrument on my leg while striking the head with the finger tips of both hands. At one particular rehearsal, the conductor asked me to hold the tambourine up and play the part by alternating the rhythms with just two fingers of one hand (as if playing the piano). This was difficult for me since I am not a pianist and did not have solid control of my fingers. I practiced it for quite some time but during the concert, the rhythms were not perfect and the conductor gave me a dissatisfied glare. After the performance, I went to his dressing room to explain that his request was not a technique percussionists use on the tambourine. His response was: "Well, you're the expert, play it your way!" The next evening, even though I played the part perfectly, he did not look up to acknowledge it. Some orchestra members shuffled their feet in support (a common practice when a member of the orchestra plays a particularly difficult solo—which, of course, this was not). In other words, they were telling the conductor to let musicians do their job.

I have undergraduate students who come to a lesson having incorrectly practiced an assignment. When this happens, I ask them to play the section again and, once more, they perform it with wrong notes. I then play the part correctly (pointing out their mistakes) and ask them *now* to play it with the right notes. What I find, however, is that once a student has practiced (or memorized) music with errors, some find it difficult to make immediate changes—an important skill for professional musicians. It's not appropriate for players to tell a conductor they will take the part home and practice it for the next rehearsal. Music students who are not able to make on-the-spot changes as requested by a teacher are probably not suited for an orchestral career.

Children who have learned to accept advice from elders fare much better in the music profession than those who constantly question everything asked of them by educators. Music and sports teach youngsters to be punctual, follow directions, and to work as team players.

Barry Green, Principal Bassist with the Cincinnati Symphony and Tennis Professional, W. Timothy Gallwey, express their thoughts about the disciplines of music and sports in *The Inner Game of Music* (Bantam Doubleday Dell Publishing Group, NY):

> *People 'play' sports and 'play' music, yet both involve hard work and discipline. Both are forms of self-expression which require a balance of spontaneity and structure, technique and inspiration. Both demand a degree of mastery over the human body, and yield immediately apparent results which can give timely feedback to the performer. Since both sports and music are commonly performed in front of an audience, they also provide an opportunity for sharing the enjoyment of excellence, as well as the experience of pressure, fears, and the excitement of ego involvement.*

Many symphony musicians become master teachers, sharing the musical skills they have acquired from years of performing the greatest music ever written with their students. As instructors, these mentors communicate a particular interpretation of the music (loud, soft, long, short, gentle, aggressive, etc.). In other words, young players learn to take directions. Many teachers will cross a student's path as they move forward in their musical education and the proper attitude for aspiring performers should be to assimilate as much information as they can from each one, eventually carving out their own ideas and techniques.

University level music students take weekly, private lessons (in many cases, with the same instructor every semester). This association builds strong student-teacher relationships and gives a professor an opportunity to observe a student's growth, not only as a performer, but as an individual. Teachers become confidants, counselors, and mentors with many relationships lasting past university life.

A good percentage of my graduates hold distinguished careers as successful performers and educators throughout the world. In fact, one of my former percussion majors, Jack Van Geem, is the Principal Percussionist of the San Francisco Symphony. The essence of the story, therefore, is: *Always be nice to your students because one day they may be your supervisor!*

There are times when music majors arrive at lessons unprepared for the week's assignment. When questioned, the most common reply is that a heavy academic load or exam preparation left them with little time to practice or that family and personal problems hindered their study. Excuses cover a wide spectrum and differ with age. My daughter, a pianist and middle-school music teacher, told me a young pupil arrived for his lesson one day, not having practiced. When she asked him why he wasn't prepared, he said: "I couldn't find the piano!" After a short discussion, the young boy explained that the house was being remodeled and the piano had been covered and moved to another room.

Excuses don't always improve with age—and even at the university level, there are students who still use variations of "the dog-ate-my-homework" justification. The biggest problem some college students have is an inability to arrive on time for lessons and/or rehearsals. Apologies range from traffic jams to not finding a parking spot, forgetting they had a lesson or a rehearsal, and sleeping late. Oversleeping is not a good excuse and if it happened once or twice, a professor might understand, but there are students who rarely arrive on time. When this becomes a major problem, I meet with them to discuss the ramifications of such a negative trait. Showing up tardy in the professional music world is an absolute "NO-NO" since orchestra rehearsals and concerts cannot begin until all musicians are onstage, in tune, and warmed up. When I have students who have trouble getting to school on time, especially for early-morning classes, I closely monitor them. The worst excuse they can give is that the alarm clock did not ring or that they slept through it. My advice for them is to buy two or three clocks and set them at varying intervals. Not only is it unacceptable to arrive late, but as students, it is also important to have eaten breakfast, to show up early, warm up, and be mentally alert.

Some pupils need to work harder than others to accomplish a well-prepared lesson and this depends on the person's musical background and natural ability. Progress is not always determined by the amount of hours one spends practicing or the individual's playing ability—it also has to do with self-image and how capable a student is in maneuvering through the hustle of college life. The road to success for those seeking a career as a professional musician entails an enormous amount of dedication, self-confidence, and natural musical abilities.

When performing in public, artists are open to criticism—not only from conductors, but also music critics and the audience. Criticism is not always easy to accept, especially when given in a derogatory manner, however, it is an accepted part of the music business. But, performers soon learn that newspaper concert reviews are, for the most part, entertainment columns and they must build a "wall" between themselves and the written word if they want to survive in this profession. The same philosophy is true for those who author a book because once it becomes public, it is also subject to criticism. Whenever students comment about a book I've written, even a simple statement such as: "Mr. Cirone, I think there are too many dynamics in this etude," I say (in a light-hearted manner), "Well, maybe you should write your own book."

As a forty-two year professor of music, I have gleaned a few insights into student behavior. There are music majors who have no other driving educational interests, such as, medicine, law, engineering, psychology, literature, etcetera. They have played a musical instrument since early childhood, been successful at it, and have a strong work ethic (mandatory in this profession). I'm convinced there is no other major course of study (at the undergraduate level) that is more demanding than music. Besides academic classes, music majors spend additional hours in ensemble practice (band, orchestra, string quartets, percussion ensemble, and brass choirs, to name a few), besides three hours (at the university level) and up to eight hours (at a conservatory) in daily practice. Yes, it's true musicians enrolled in a performance degree program can practice up to eight hours a day! When I entered The Juilliard School in 1959 (a conservatory), a counselor told me I had to set aside a minimum of three hours a day for practice, including weekends (in those days, we got off easy). Rehearsals and performances outside of school (community orchestras, dance bands, church services, youth orchestras, jazz clubs, and weddings) also add to a musician's playing schedule.

After teaching for twenty years, I began to notice that more and more of my students did not have the same diligence and motivation as the earlier generation. I wondered what caused this change and came up with a theory I call: The demise of the paper route. As a twelve-year-old boy, I woke up every morning at 4:00 a.m., rode my bike to pick up the newspapers, folded and packed them in my bag, and then delivered them to customers seven days a week. Every Saturday afternoon I went to each subscriber's home to collect the weekly fee. After paying for the papers, the remaining money was mine. This experience taught me responsibility, honesty, dedication, hard work, and personal satisfaction. In other words, I learned it paid to work hard.

Today, it's rare to see teenagers delivering newspapers on bicycles. Adults have taken over these jobs, distributing the daily news by car, and depriving youngsters with an opportunity to develop good work ethics. Many households also employ gardeners, housekeepers, and nannies, leaving adolescents with even fewer chores and commitments. And, now that music and sports programs have been cut back or eliminated from schools, it is even more difficult for children to find ways to develop the necessary skills for acquiring the rewards of hard work and accountability.

Some university students soon realize they are not cut out for a performing career while others stay the course even if music is not their ultimate goal. In fact, majoring in music is not such a bad idea for an undergraduate because the discipline required for this major transfers to other professions. Taking on a project (assigned lesson) and preparing it for a weekly presentation (for an instructor) trains students to complete an activity in a short period of time with immediate feedback.

I taught at Stanford University in California for almost ten years and during one departmental meeting, the Music Chair shared a talk he had with the Director of Admissions regarding incoming freshmen. A question arose about how to select the best qualified applicants from so many excellent candidates in all disciplines. It is important to note that Stanford performing ensembles recruit undergraduates who are usually not music majors but have studied an instrument and want to perform while at school. Consequently, it's necessary that a certain number of entering freshmen have a musical background in order to fill positions within the orchestra and band. So, the Chair of the Music Department said to the Director of Admissions: "If two entering freshmen have the identical grade-point average, community-service record, and so forth, and one of them is a musician, that candidate will be the better student." His point was that musicians develop a highly-disciplined life style that carries over into other fields of study.

Charles Reid quotes Sir John Barbirolli, the celebrated European conductor, on the subject of work ethics in *John Barbirolli* (Hamish Hamilton LTD, London):

> *I like to take some time off from conducting and stay at home working and studying without having to answer the telephone and without going out at all except for a drive to some place I want to see or for a little picnic, if we're staying in the country, I call that heaven. I don't call it a holiday. I've never been on a holiday in my life. The thought of holiday disturbs me.*
> *"You have something against holidays?" he was asked. I find them disturbing, depressing. I was like that, or nearly like it as a child. We used to go for our fortnight to Brighton. I used to beg to be allowed to take my cello with me.*

*"And they let you take it?" Oh, yes, because they knew of my fear, a kind of fear, of being idle . . . I have that fear still. Between concerts I **must** study and rehearse. If I have one rehearsal in a day I can enjoy the rest of it. Evelyn says that with one rehearsal a day, I'm 'bearable'. . . This is something I don't boast about. I think it's reprehensible. But there you are.*

Students who excel as music majors at the undergraduate level and want to pursue graduate-level studies in this field love to perform and have no other strong interest. It certainly is not because a career as a professional musician guarantees them a job at graduation. This is not to imply that there are guarantees of employment for other majors, but certainly more opportunities exist outside the music field. Graduating music majors interested in pursuing an orchestral position have to wait (sometimes years) to prepare for and qualify as audition candidates for a major orchestra. Performance majors, consequently, become freelance musicians, playing in a myriad of musical ensembles, honing their audition skills while making a living.

Since there is such a large number of music majors seeking careers as professional musicians (with relatively few available positions), the glamour of performing with a major orchestra has waned. This has caused many university music schools to concentrate on education degrees and freelance careers. The problem, as

I see it, is such a course of study is diluted and students are not able to attain the level of proficiency required to be competitive as classically-trained musicians. This is particularly evident with percussion majors. In lieu of a comprehensive program of orchestral repertoire, many schools now stress world music, drum set, solo marimba, steel pan, African drumming, and a variety of ethnic hand drums. I, therefore, advise instrumental music students to enroll in a conservatory of music in order to master the skills necessary for performing in a major orchestra.

I believe training young musicians (even education majors) to perform orchestral literature from the Classical and Romantic Periods provides them with skills that carry over into other concentrations. Studying the compositions of these great composers not only increases one's awareness of the grandeur of our Western European tradition, but includes the study of classical music forms (sonata allegro, rondo, fugue, theme and variations, etc.), a depth of musical enrichment, technical proficiency, orchestration, development of harmonic and melodic concepts, contemporary rhythmic advances and, above all, a love for the greatest music ever written.

Considering the actual number of musicians needed for wind and percussion positions in a major United States orchestra (4 trumpets, 3 trombones, 5 percussionists, 4 clarinets, 3 flutes, 2 oboes, 1 English horn, 3 bassoons, 4 French horns, 1 tuba, 1 harp, and 1 piano), it seems more likely that a college athlete will be able to secure a job with a major league sports team than a music student to win an audition as a member of a major symphony orchestra.

And, athletes can be trained to play a number of positions on a sports team whereas musicians are only qualified to perform on a single instrument.

Orchestral performers exist in a world of foreign language terms. Most composers use Italian when adding musical directives to a score. German composers use German and some Italian. French composers use French and also some Italian. Aspiring musicians, therefore, are encouraged to study Italian, German, and French to meet the challenges of comprehending foreign language directives in musical scores. Without a working knowledge of these languages, students must commit foreign musical terms to memory or look them up in a music dictionary. The most prevalent language of study today is Spanish but, unfortunately, Spanish is not used for musical directives and even Latin American composers use Italian terms. Composers use these terms for specific instructions as to how they want their compositions performed, for example, tempo markings (fast, slow, moderate, accelerating or slowing down), dynamics (very soft, soft, moderately loud, loud, very loud), and character indications (majestic, gentle, expressive, sonorous, aggressive, with spirit, in a military style, graceful, mysterious)—the list is endless and can be found in all three languages. To this end, my first project after retirement was to compile an exhaustive musical dictionary in Italian, French, and German—*Cirone's Pocket Dictionary of Foreign*

Musical Terms (Meredith Music Publications, Galesville, MD). The book also includes percussion terms not found in standard musical dictionaries and a listing of many string terms composers use in scores and conductors request from the podium.

Daniel Barenboim, the internationally-renown pianist and conductor, describes the importance of understanding foreign musical terms in his biography: *A Life in Music* (Charles Scribner's Sons, Macmillan Publishing Company, NY):

> *It always fascinates me that musicians, whenever they feel the need for a slight modification of dynamic, will, nine times out of ten, slow down to obtain greater expression. Many musicians have no hesitation in getting slower but would never dream of going faster. It is important to understand that the terminology employed in music—which stems mainly from Italian or German—really means something: the words have a definite significance, which can be analysed. Rubato, for instance, means 'stolen', and when you have stolen something, you have to give it back!*
>
> *Musically speaking, this means that if you take your time over something to make it more expressive, you must 'return' that time at some point. Modification, flexibility and fluctuation of tempo must be related to metrical strictness. In an ideal situation, when a rubato takes place over three or four bars, then over eight bars or sixteen bars, or whatever the metric pattern is, the loss of tempo should be compensated for, so that if you put on the metronome at the beginning of the sixteen bars and play around it freely, you should, at the end of the sixteen bars, be back level with it.*

There are many performing musicians who never win symphony auditions but still remain in the music business. I present master classes throughout the United States on a number of musical topics, but the one I consider to be of utmost importance is *Careers in Music*. Students enroll in colleges and universities to prepare themselves for a specific vocation. As a professor, I believe it is part of my obligation to steer them in a direction that will fulfill their goals. I, therefore, encourage my pupils to think "outside the box" when it comes to making a living in this profession. My suggestion to those pursuing a career as an orchestral musician and have not won an audition (or made it into the finals) within five years after graduation, is to begin thinking about a change in direction. I use the following outline to stimulate ideas and suggest to those with a music degree that they can find employment in three main areas: Performance, Education, and Related Fields.

There is no particular hierarchy to this listing except that the first two categories (Performance and Education) have been organized (with some exceptions) from the most stable to the least secure (in terms of salary, benefits, pension, vacation, and tenure). The last three positions in the Performance category (Conductor, Arranger, and Composer) are not necessarily at the bottom of the wage and benefit scale since some of these musicians are very successful and demand high compensation; but, on the average, there are more conductors, arrangers, and composers who spend their lives trying to attain such prominent status, but never do.

Performance

Symphony Orchestra (full time, good salary & benefits)

Opera (part time, good salary & benefits)

Military Bands (good career with early retirement)

Ballet (short season, good pay & benefits)

Recording Studio, Movies (good pay if steady work)

Jazz Artist (pay varies with long-term or weekend club dates

Freelance Player (no paid benefits)

Musical Theater (good pay for successful Broadway shows)

Community or Part-Time Orchestras (freelance work)

Road Bands (success depends on popularity of lead singer)

Casuals, Weddings (freelance work)

Concert Soloist (excellent fees)

Cruise Ships (not suggested for long-term commitment)

Young Audience Concerts (freelance work)

Amusement Theme Parks (low pay with no future)

Conductor (great career for those who rise to the top)

Composer (few can live off royalties)

Arranger (pays well if steady work)

Education

University/College

Jr. College

Primary and Secondary Education

Conservatory (most are part-time positions)

Middle School Music Specialist

*All of the above can be full time with good pay & benefits

Private Music Teacher (supplemental income)

Artist-in-Resident (good pay if full-time university position)

Music Store Teacher (low pay, no benefits)

Related Fields

Manufacturing (good pay & benefits in product design)

Publishing (editors & music engravers—usually part time)

Orchestra Librarian (excellent position with major orchestras)

Copyist, Music Engraver, Editor (part time with no benefits)

Instrument Repair and Design (small-business potential)

Artist Representative/Agent (small-business potential)

Sales, Marketing, Education, Artist Relations (good salary & benefits)

League of American Orchestras, Management/Intern (can lead to full-time position in major orchestras)

Orchestra Personnel Manager (if full time, good pay & benefits)

American Federation of Music Official (full time, good pay & benefits)

Music Critic, Journalism (usually part time)

Music Therapist (good pay & benefits)

Performing Arts Administrator (good pay & benefits)

On-Line Publishing (self publish)

Recording Engineer/Producer (business opportunity)

Musical Arts Fund Raiser (good pay & benefits)

Customer Relations (full time with manufacturers)

Retail Music Store (business opportunity)

Years ago, I presented this lecture at a Ludwig Percussion Symposium at the University of Austin, Texas. After discussing possible job opportunities for musicians, Bill Ludwig, III, President of the Ludwig Drum Company at that time and a sponsor for the Symposium, raised his hand to make a comment. "Tony," he said, "You forgot one thing—you have to get a break!" Bill's statement was so true. We all need help to reach our goals. And, not only are opportunities important, but we have to be ready and willing to take them when they come. I've had students who, for one reason or another, have not taken advantage of a serious job offer and, in some cases, it was the only one they had in their entire musical careers.

At times, a position requires a move out of state or even the country but it can jump-start a career. And, when that job is offered, all those endless hours of practice, sight reading, study, last-minute rehearsals, playing without remuneration, and subbing, pays off. A break can come from a colleague, teacher, trade magazine, at a convention, or through the audition process. I suggest to students who have graduated from a university or conservatory to consider taking lessons from members of major orchestras and to try and get on the substitute list. Performing as an "extra" is not only a fantastic way to gain experience, but it looks great on a résumé.

I was fortunate to have had a number of breaks in my career. An important one occurred when I was a Junior at Lyndhurst High School. I won the audition as First Snare Drum Player for the New Jersey State Honor Orchestra. This experience opened up the world of orchestral music to me and spearheaded my career as a percussionist. I still remember the first composition the orchestra rehearsed, *Lincoln Portrait* by Aaron Copland.

The next big break occurred during my third year at The Juilliard School. Gar Whaley, a good friend and colleague, and I decided to collaborate on writing a snare drum book. It was during the same summer I married my wife (another break). She worked in Manhattan so I was left with a lot of free time to develop the manuscript. Although there were plenty of snare drum methods on the market, most of them taught a marching or rudimental-drumming approach that did not reflect the orchestral training I was receiving at the conservatory.

My idea was to compose etudes that used musical forms, dynamics, articulations, and directives so prevalent in orchestral music. By the end of the summer, I had written fifty snare drum etudes—in other words, the entire book! I was embarrassed to tell Gar what I had done but he accepted it and went on to complete his own, *Rhythmic Patterns of Contemporary Music* (Joel Rothman Publications).

I now had the task of finding a publisher; so, with manuscript in hand, I went to Chappell & Company because they had the rights to the famous *Modern School for Snare Drum* by Morris Goldenberg. Even though I didn't have an appointment, I spoke to a representative who said the company was happy with Goldenberg's publication and did not want to add another snare drum book to their catalog. Undaunted, I tried my luck with a smaller company, Music for Percussion, who concentrated on percussion music and new contemporary compositions. They liked what I had done but said it would take five years before they could get it on their publishing schedule. At twenty-two years of age, it sounded like an eternity—so, I walked out.

My big break came at the next stop, Henry Adler's Drum Shop, located in the heart of Times Square. It was a well-known store to drummers because it had excellent teachers and Adler was also a publisher. He offered me a two-year contract for the book I had entitled, *Portraits in Rhythm*; but, he changed it to *50 Studies for Snare Drum*.

During this two-year waiting period, I was offered the percussion position with the San Francisco Symphony and moved to the West Coast with my family. Before long, the published copy was in the mail from a company called Belwin-Mills Publications (with the original title, *Portraits in Rhythm*). And, although I had never heard of this publisher, I later found out they had bought Henry Adler Publications, including all of his outstanding contracts.

In reality, this was a very big break for me since Belwin-Mills was one of the largest music-education publishers in the world. They changed the title back to *Portraits in Rhythm*, but included *50 Studies for Snare Drum* as a subtitle. It quickly caught on with percussion educators and began to sell worldwide within a few years. It is still a best seller and has become a standard text for training snare drummers throughout the international community. Years later, I wrote an analysis for the original fifty etudes (*Portraits in Rhythm*) in a new publication, entitled *Portraits in Rhythm Study Guide* (Alfred Publishing Company, CA). At this writing, it has been translated into Spanish.

The next important step in my career came during my fourth year at Juilliard. Saul Goodman, (my teacher and Timpanist of the New York Philharmonic), selected three students to audition for the xylophone part in Saint-Saëns *Carnival of the Animals* for one of Leonard Bernstein's *Young People's Concerts* with the New York Philharmonic. Ironically, his assistant conductor, Seiji Ozawa, was assigned to hear the audition. He later became a music director for whom I would work with the San Francisco Symphony. What a break to have been selected to perform this concert, conducted by Leonard Bernstein and the New York Philharmonic at Carnegie Hall, for the televised series and subsequent CD release (Sony: *Bernstein Century Children's Classics*).

It is also advantageous for musicians to seek sponsorships from leading instrument manufacturers because they offer valuable networking opportunities and provide monetary support for endorsing their products during master classes and clinics. I have been an endorser for the Zildjian Cymbal Company, Yamaha Corporation, and Remo Drum Company since my early years as a professional.

To summarize, discipline, team spirit, and breaks are important, but *nothing* insures success for an aspiring artist more than a strong work ethic. The best orchestras in the world are comprised of highly-trained musicians who know how to get to Carnegie Hall where their performances are reviewed by highly-respected music critics. I think most musicians would agree that this is the height of accomplishment within the orchestral world. And, if they were asked how they got there, I'm sure they would respond: *Practice, Practice, Practice!*

THE ULTIMATE INTERVIEW

*Throughout my career, nervousness and stage-fright have
never left me before playing. And each of the thousands of concerts I have played at, I feel as bad as I did the very first time.*

—Pablo Casals

The audition process for a position in a major symphony
orchestra is incredibly involved; in fact, it can be downright
discouraging, and to complicate matters even more, requirements
differ among orchestras (although the basic premise is similar). The
American Federation of Musicians advertises openings throughout the world in *The International Musician* newsletter. Qualified
applicants submit a cover letter and résumé to potential employ-
ers by a determined date. The Audition Committee is comprised
of approximately ten members, most of whom come from the section in which the opening occurs, that is, string players for a string
position, trumpets, trombones, and French horns for brass openings, and so forth. Rules require that a certain number of first chair
(Principal) or titled (Associate and Assistant Principal) musicians
also serve on this committee.

The method for selecting candidates begins with the audition committee who reviews all résumés (which can number up

to three hundred for one opening). Candidates who do not demonstrate professional experience as members or substitute players with an orchestra may be disqualified. If the opening is for a titled or first-chair position, applicants may not even be invited unless they have been a member of a *major* orchestra. Actual performing experience, consequently, is of utmost importance. A university degree or study with a distinguished professor does not necessarily qualify an applicant entrance into the audition process. The most important criteria is onstage experience. It is crucial, however, that potential candidates consider taking lessons with musicians from major symphony orchestras since they can provide them with the expertise and knowledge of the repertoire needed to win an audition.

In the past, the music director made most of the decisions regarding the selection of candidates for open chairs, but orchestra members became disappointed with the quality of some of their appointments. The following quote is taken from a 1974 report by the San Francisco Symphony Players' Committee:

> . . . *there were instances of hiring that showed these conductors' standards to be capricious and even dangerous to the orchestra.*

As a result, the audition procedure was drastically changed. Orchestra members now demand equal say in the selection of candidates and although this system has gone through many permutations, the following describes the most current method used by the San Francisco Symphony for screening applicants.

After reviewing all résumés, the committee selects thirty to sixty qualified musicians. Some audition procedures require candidates to submit an audio CD or video DVD of specific orchestral repertoire before being invited to perform in person. Since sound quality is of utmost importance, many players use the services of professional recording studios.

Some contracts allow a music director to designate a predetermined number of musicians to move directly into the semi-final rounds. These players are not required to submit a recording or to take the preliminary audition. This is also true for current orchestra members who want to "move up" to a better chair—they, too, proceed directly to the semi-final rounds. Auditionees selected to appear in person are notified by mail and pay their own travel, hotel, and food expenses.

If more than thirty candidates are invited, the committee usually splits into two groups. Individual auditions take from ten to twenty minutes with all musicians performing the same preselected, published list of excerpts. Candidates must pass the preliminary round with a majority of "yes" votes in order to move into the semi-final rounds—both of which are held, without exception, behind a partition. Musicians perform onstage without the distraction of dividers, giving them as natural a setting as possible, while the committee sits behind a screen in the concert hall. In the past, women were not permitted to wear high-heeled shoes because the sound could be considered a source of discrimination. The San Francisco Symphony has now placed a carpeted runner onstage to alleviate this problem. Candidates are not allowed to talk during an audition and are referred to by number. Those who fail to abide by these rules, and identify themselves in some way, are dismissed. A performer can be asked to repeat a passage of music, play it slower, faster, or with different articulation, and the committee can stop the process at any time to say they have heard enough (which can be a positive or a negative directive).

Those who receive a majority of "yes" votes are passed into one or more semi-final rounds that continue until there are approximately three to six remaining players—these musicians then proceed to the final round. At the conclusion of the semi-finals, if the audition committee decides there are no qualified candidates, the process ends.

The final rounds can take place immediately, the following day, or players can be invited to return at a future time (with all expenses paid by the orchestra). The music director enters the audition process during the final round. The San Francisco Symphony uses a screen for the first hearing, but after that, the music director has the option to observe performers even though the committee continues to remain behind the screen. If an ensemble round is requested (the player is asked to perform within the section in which the opening occurs), the screen is taken down. Voting at this time also varies with orchestras. Although the audition committee passes qualified candidates, the final decision for selecting a winner is made at the sole discretion of the music director.

Methods for selecting finalists used in the past were with a point system. In other words, a player had to receive a certain amount of points from both the committee and the music director in order to win an audition. This system, however, could be weighed in the music director's favor (depending on how points are distributed). For instance, the maestro might have a total of 150 points and the committee, a total of 100 points. If a candidate needed 200 points to qualify, the music director could simply vote less than 100 points to disqualify the applicant. In other words, it did not matter how many points the committee gave a candidate since the combined score would not total the necessary 200 points to win. On the other hand, the audition committee could vote less than 50 points to disqualify a candidate. Today, most voting is done by a majority of "yes" or "no" votes and not through a point system.

The music director can prolong the audition process by hiring a few finalists to perform a complete series of rehearsals and concerts (one or two weeks) with the orchestra to further evaluate the musician's abilities, intonation, and interaction within the section in which the opening occurs. This process can take months. When this occurs, candidates receive a salary, travel, and hotel expenses. If the music director is not satisfied with any of the finalists, the procedure ends and a new audition is scheduled (usually) within six to twelve months.

Auditions are an extremely arduous experience. Those who do not pass the preliminary round return home. Candidates that pass may have to wait hours or days for the semi-final rounds to be completed. It's hard to imagine a more stress-filled environment. Only the most secure players, those who continually perform at a high level of proficiency, are able to pass through these repeated cycles.

When a winner is finally selected, he or she performs with the orchestra as a probationary member for two years. The first year of employment is called the Audition Year.

String players, who win an audition for a chair near the back of a section, perform for one or two weeks on the first or second stand within their respective sections (violin I, violin II, viola, cello, bass) so the music director can closely observe them.

If a candidate passes the audition year with approval from both the review committee and the music director, the player is hired as a probationary member for the second season. If the probationary member passes the review committee at the end of the second season, it then becomes the sole decision of the music director as to whether or not to hire the musician as a tenured member of the orchestra.

It is significantly more difficult to select musicians for one of the more exposed principal positions (violin, viola, cello, bass, flute, oboe, clarinet, bassoon, trumpet, trombone, tuba, timpani, percussion, piano, and harp) because first-chair players function as soloists. When selecting candidates for a principal position, a conductor takes into consideration the personality of the player's sound; consequently, some of these exposed chairs remain vacant for up to ten years and must be temporarily filled by promoting a member of the section to that position.

The concertmaster is *not* hired through the audition process but is directly appointed by the music director since he or she works so closely with the conductor to achieve the correct balance, phrasing, and interpretation of the music. The concertmaster also consults with the conductor regarding bowing decisions. Although this is not a tenured position, if a previously-tenured orchestra member assumes the position of concertmaster and is subsequently dismissed, he or she is entitled to return to the orchestra as a tenured member in the first violin section.

The current base salary for entering musicians in major orchestras is more than $100 thousand per annum. The San Francisco Symphony states that compensation for the associate concertmaster and all principal chairs shall not be less than 20% above base salary. Assistant concertmasters, associate principals, and assistant principals are paid no less than 10% above base salary—but, maximum salary amounts are open to negotiation for all orchestra members no matter what chair they hold. There is no salary range stated for the concertmaster, however, as mentioned earlier, this position is usually the highest paid member of an orchestra.

Symphony benefits include medical, dental, life insurance, sick leave, vacation (approximately ten weeks a year), option weeks (up to five without pay), seniority pay (approximately $100 to $200 a week), sabbatical leave (three or six months every seven years), touring per diem, radio broadcast fees, and a pension plan. Orchestra members do not accrue vacation time and even first-year probationary players receive the same ten weeks as tenured musicians—eight of which take place when the orchestra is not performing. The other two weeks are "floating vacation weeks" and can be taken at any time during the season. A position in a major symphony orchestra is considered a very secure job within the music industry and that's one reason why so many applicants apply for one opening.

There are musicians who do not pass the probationary process because of reasons, such as, musicianship, sound, rhythm, or intonation. If a music director suspects there are concerns with a probationary member's performance, the contract requires that he or she meet privately with the individual to discuss these specific areas. The probationary member is first given written notice regarding the music director and/or committee's comments and at least two meetings take place before a notice of termination can be issued.

Committee members and a music director can disagree on a candidate's abilities since it is an educated opinion among highly-trained professionals. There have been many candidates who have not won auditions with the San Francisco Symphony but have gone on to careers with other orchestras. The following story has been documented by music critics and the San Francisco Symphony Players' Committee.

An extreme example of the probationary process occurred when Roland Kohloff, Principal Timpanist, accepted the same position with the New York Philharmonic. This move created an opening in San Francisco and as with all principal chairs, the timpanist is an important player. The audition was announced and the process began. In the end, however, the committee was not satisfied with any of the finalists but, Seiji Ozawa, the music director at the time, gave his full support to one candidate, Elayne Jones, who had extensive experience as a member of the American Symphony Orchestra in New York, conducted by Leopold Stokowski. She was, therefore, offered the position.

The procedure, at that time, was to take a vote after the candidate played with the orchestra for two years. When Ms. Jones came up for tenure, along with seven other candidates, the players' committee met with the music director to review which musicians should be considered for tenured positions. After separate discussions for each candidate, committee members voted by secret ballot. Each of the seven members of the committee cast votes from 1 to 100 points. In order to qualify for tenure, the candidate had to score 351 of the possible 700 points. Fewer than 351 points resulted in dismissal at the end of the season. More than 351 points qualified the player to pass on to the music director for a final vote.

The first six players passed both the committee and Ozawa's vote and were granted tenure. Two of the most visible positions, Principal Timpani (Elayne Jones) and Principal Bassoon (Ryohei Nakagawa) were then voted on by the committee. The first vote was for Ms. Jones who did not pass (the committee voted less than 351 points). The music director, therefore, did not have a vote and the candidate was dismissed. Ozawa accepted the committee's decision. But when he learned they also rejected Nakagawa for the principal bassoon position, Ozawa eventually demanded that both Jones and Nakagawa be granted tenure.

The following quote is taken from the 1974 report to the ICSOM (International Conference of Symphony and Opera Musicians) Convention by the San Francisco Symphony Players' Committee:

> *This has to be emphasized: Seiji Ozawa did not disagree with the Committee's decision regarding Elayne Jones. At no time did he ask the Committee to reconsider their vote about her, as he did with Nakagawa. At no time did he express to the Committee either a strong personal or musical regret that Miss Jones had not been granted tenure—as he did with Nakagawa. During meetings and discussions spanning three days, Maestro Ozawa several times asked the Committee to re-vote the decision regarding Mr. Nakagawa, but he never asked the same action for Miss Jones. He said more than once that he could accept the Jones decision.*

When the media got hold of the news, they ran with it in local newspapers. San Francisco Chronicle, May 21, 1974, Music Critic, Robert Commanday:

> *The decisions against Elayne Jones and Ryohei Nakagawa were preposterous, scandalous. In intonation, tone and rhythm, the timpani playing of Miss Jones has been one of the symphony's strongest new elements, giving it an accurate rhythm structure with a decisiveness that lent security to particularly crucial performances by guest and opera conductors. The timpanist is the third most important player, after the Concertmaster and Principal Oboe.*

San Francisco Chronicle, May 22, 1974, Herb Caen's Column:

> *It's only Wednesday, but we have our Quote of the Week. It comes from a member of the S. F. Symphony committee that voted, astonishingly, to deny tenure to two star members, Timpanist Elayne Jones, only black member of the orchestra, and First Bassoonist Ryohei Nakagawa. "Our decision proves we aren't racist," says this committee person. "If we had voted to retain them just because one is black and the other Oriental, THAT would have been racist."*

San Francisco Examiner, May 23, 1974, Music Critic, Alexander Fried (this quote was included in a review of Schoenberg's *Gurrelieder*):

> *Exercising a power no symphony contract should have assigned to it, the seven-player committee ousted timpanist Elayne Jones and first bassoon Ryohei Nakagawa from their expected chances of job tenure. Such a committee should be advisory, but not fire and hire. . . . But anyone observing Miss Jones' kettledrum performance, with its continual distinction and perfection, was bound to see she was just about as important to the music as even the magnificent solo singers.*

The committee's vote, however, was sanctioned by the American Federation of Musicians Union Local 6 and was conducted according to contract regulations so nothing could be done to overturn it.

The charge of racism emerged as quoted in the San Francisco Examiner on May 24, 1974, by Music Critic, Arthur Bloomfield:

> *In the wake of an extremely misguided and lamentable sacking of two star San Francisco Symphony players—through a curious action of the orchestra's seven-man Players' Committee—these things have come to pass:*
>
> - *An outraged concertgoer came up with a petition of 108 names decrying the ousting of tympanist Elayne Jones and bassoonist Ryohei Nakagawa.*
>
> - *The Symphony management began to receive letters from subscribers threatening to withdraw financial support if Miss Jones and Nakagawa who were denied tenure are not reinstated.*
>
> - *"Kick Racism out of Art" said another patron's placard.*
>
> - *But . . .* [the petition] *made no mention of color and one's tempted to believe that the motives of the committee in vetoing the two players were not consciously or overtly related to matters of race.*

Alice Yarish, Journalist for the San Francisco Examiner, shared her point of view in the August 22-28, 1974, Sunday Magazine:

The critics and their coterie of supporters in the music world have charged the committee with "racism and sexism," and Miss Jones has filed suit against the Symphony Association and Local 6 of the Musicians Union on the same charge. Jones happens to be a black woman, Nakagawa a Japanese man.

So, what really happened? Why were the two musicians denied tenure? Was it due to racial and sexual bias on the part of the committee, as some say? Or was it because they failed in musicianship as most orchestra members say? Far be it from me to make a musical judgment.

Look at the charge of sexism. The San Francisco Symphony Orchestra has 22 women players, more than any other major orchestra either in the United States or Europe. As to racism, the conductor himself is, of course, Japanese, and there are and have been in the past players of many races and nationalities— black, Japanese, Filipino, Latins.

Ms. Jones' lawsuit against the orchestra was eventually dismissed. Nakagawa accepted the committee's vote and left the orchestra. Jones played with the Symphony for another year until litigation was concluded and continued to hold the position of timpanist with the San Francisco Opera.

There were many letters to the Symphony from patrons and supporters of the arts, expressing their anger and disappointment with the orchestra's decision not to renew Jones and Nakagawa's contracts. They voiced their delight with both musicians and couldn't understand how the players' committee would not grant tenure to such outstanding performers. But, it's difficult for patrons of the arts to understand the extraordinary level of detail that comes into play when deciding whether or not to hire musicians on a permanent basis. These decisions revolve around subtleties of intonation, phrasing, sound production, rhythm, and articulation—all important elements considered for granting tenure.

The audition process was agreed to by management and the music director. The vote, therefore, was legally binding and no language in the contract allowed the decision to be rescinded. New auditions were scheduled for both positions.

My own audition story began while I was a student at The Juilliard School. I tried out for the Baltimore Symphony Orchestra and the Boston Symphony during my senior year, both of which gave me valuable experience for my next opportunity. Saul Goodman sent me to Carnegie Hall to audition for George Szell, conductor of the Cleveland Symphony Orchestra. He stood on the podium and I performed in the percussion section (alone) towards the back of the stage. Maestro Szell asked me to play the famous two-measure snare drum part to Maurice Ravel's *Bolero*, commonly used at percussion auditions. It begins as a solo and continues at an extremely soft dynamic for many measures before making a great *crescendo*. Generally, conductors allow audition candidates to per-form this excerpt by themselves to be sure they know the correct tempo and dynamic, but Szell raised his baton and conducted as though we were playing with an orchestra.

When I perform this solo at an actual concert, I watch the conductor for the beginning tempo and, then, intently listen to the rhythm of the basses, concentrating on evenly articulating each note (very difficult at such a soft dynamic). During an actual performance, however, it's not necessary to watch the conductor since there is no change of tempo—but I was the only musician onstage, so I didn't take my eyes off Szell. As it turned out, this was a defining moment. After a few measures, he increased the tempo and then slowed it down, challenging me to follow him without distorting the rhythm. Evidently he was pleased with my performance because he invited me to play at the final audition in Cleveland at the orchestra's expense. Although I did not win the position, it gave me confidence to know I had been selected for the finals.

I was very fortunate to have studied at The Juilliard School with Saul Goodman since he was a major force in placing timpanists and percussionists in orchestras throughout the world. Whenever a conductor came to town, looking for a timpanist or a percussionist for his orchestra, Goodman arranged a private meeting at Carnegie Hall for his students. Of course, this was before current audition procedures when conductors were able to select musicians without a committee.

Josef Krips, Music Director of the San Francisco Symphony, had called Goodman years earlier, asking him to recommend a timpanist. Goodman said: "I have the perfect candidate for the job!" Roland Kohloff assumed that position and played with the orchestra for sixteen years before being hired by the New York Philharmonic—ironically, replacing his teacher, Saul Goodman, who had retired.

Several years later, Krips again called Goodman, this time to request a percussionist. And, once again, Saul said: "I have the perfect candidate for the job!" He sent me to Krips' Manhattan hotel room. When I arrived, the maestro said in his heavy German accent: "So, you *vant* to play with the San Francisco Symphony Orchestra?" I replied, very nervously, "Yes, Maestro." Two weeks later I had a contract in the mail.

Securing a position with a major orchestra (by invitation or audition) is just the first step in a long process for gaining tenure. As previously mentioned, a two-year probationary period is required so the music director and audition committee can observe the musician's performance to be able to arrive at a final decision. During the first week of my probationary period, I played the triangle part to Brahms' *Haydn Variations*. My usual technique was to add a follow-through, upward motion after the beater struck the instrument. Krips evidently liked what I had done because at a subsequent rehearsal (with no percussion, so I wasn't onstage), a colleague told me he asked the string players to end a certain phrase with "more flair like our new triangle player." One never knows what impresses (or turns off) a conductor.

That same year we were rehearsing *Don Juan* by Richard Strauss, a famous composition often performed by orchestras. I was assigned the orchestra bell part that has a beautiful solo, ending with two notes, C# and F#. At this point, Krips stopped the orchestra and said to me: "My Dear, this is where the Gates of Heaven open up." That's all he said and continued to rehearse the section. I was dumbfounded.

When a conductor addresses a musician regarding a passage, he generally offers a suggestion as to what he wants, that is, faster, slower, louder, softer, but he gave me no indication as to what he was looking for except that the Gates had better open. I thought to myself: "Oh my God, they didn't teach me this at Juilliard!" As the orchestra approached these two powerful notes, I remembered something Goodman repeatedly said: "You have to play with *schmaltz*." I never really knew what *schmaltz* meant, but I did know it had something to do with show business. So, when the orchestra arrived at this measure, I looked directly at Krips and made a flowing, graceful, upward motion with my hand as the mallet struck the instrument. He looked back at me and smiled, and I thought: "Thank God, the Gates of Heaven must have opened!"

A conductor is not the only one who creates a visual, onstage presence, musicians also influence the listening audience. Within the string sections, as mentioned earlier, some players move dramatically, adding to the audience's perception of the music's emotional content. As a professor of music, I can say this is not an easy concept to teach to students because it falls into the category of natural ability. While it can be distracting if overdone, no body movement is equally disconcerting. Concert soloists display these gestures to a greater degree than orchestral musicians because of the dramatic content of their solo lines.

In my years of coaching students, the topic of how to express musical phrases with body movement would regularly be discussed because of its inherent connection to communicating musical directives—such as, *dolce* (sweetly), *cantabile* (in a singing style), *con calore* (with warmth), *passionato* (with emotion), *sentito* (with feeling), and *expressivo* (with expression). The difference between *pp* (very soft) and *subito pp* (suddenly very soft) cannot be interpreted without the use of some body language. The essential details of sweetly, warmth, emotion, feeling, and the articulation of normal passionate musicianship are enhanced when musicians transmit these emotions through visible and expressive use of the hands, arms, and general movement of the upper body. Teaching this concept, however, is another matter since there are no particular movements connected to any one emotion. All performers articulate body movement differently and with more or less exaggeration.

The use of body language should be natural; so, if I detect a lack of visible involvement with the music, I encourage students to use simple actions by helping performers relax and move their body with the phrases. It's possible that some musicians who pursue careers as members of a symphony orchestra may experience difficulty winning auditions if they are not able to demonstrate the music's emotional content through body movement and the expressive use of hands and arms while playing.

Goodman dramatically drummed into his students (pardon the pun) three words at The Juilliard School: Precision, Sensitivity, Musicality. Precision refers to technique, because without a solid command of technical proficiency on an instrument and rhythmic accuracy when performing, there is no sense in going any further. Once the goal of precision has been met, he preached the merits of playing with sensitivity (passion and excitement). When these two elements come together, the result is musicality—what Goodman expected at every lesson.

An extraordinary amount of detail must transpire for a performance to take place and the continuous interactions that occur between a conductor and musicians (during rehearsals and concerts) create a plethora of never-ending variations of classical repertoire. The subtleties musicians are able to produce with just one single note are endless, not to mention the phrasing possibilities of long musical lines. How can a performer explain the methods they use to create the musical directives of anger, sadness, joy, misery, passion, aggression, serenity, and rage? It's not possible through language—rather, it is an expression of the mind, working through the physical senses. At a final audition, when there is no screen separating the player from the conductor, these attributes are mandatory. Music directors are not only looking for technical proficiency, but also for demonstrations of expressive qualities that communicate artistry and passion during *The Ultimate Interview.*

THE MUSIC DIRECTOR

There is no form of occupation which has a worse effect on
a man's character than that of a conductor.

—Walter Legge

During my years with the San Francisco Symphony, I performed under Music Directors: Josef Krips and Seiji Ozawa (seven years each); Edo de Waart (eight years); Herbert Blomstedt (ten years); and I retired under the baton of Michael Tilson Thomas (four years). At this writing, Michael is in his sixteenth year with the orchestra. I consider myself very privileged to have played with such a diversity of music directors, considering the fact that some musicians have only worked with one music director for their entire careers. Eugene Ormandy conducted the Philadelphia Orchestra from 1936 to 1980, a forty-four year tenure, longer than most symphony players work with an orchestra. In my opinion, it would be difficult to sustain inspired performances with one maestro for such a long period of time. It's not only refreshing for musicians to perform under music directors with different conducting techniques, but orchestras and patrons alike also need to be exposed to new repertoire and contrasting interpretations that various conductors provide. I was fortunate to have had an opportunity to perform with

Ormandy when he guest conducted the San Francisco Symphony after his retirement from Philadelphia. Guest conductors tend to program their preferred compositions and *Pictures at an Exhibition* by Mussorgsky was, by far, one of his favorites. I can still remember Ormandy's unique and well-thought-out interpretation to this day.

A lot has been written about the qualifications a conductor should possess with regard to leading an orchestra, from baton technique, intonation, balance, tempo, and phrasing, to communication, rapport, and charisma. Most musicians agree that these all come under the responsibility of a conductor. Yet, other important qualities are needed that are not so easily put into words. This "something else" falls under the categories of intuition, feeling, sensitivity, and soul; yet, to translate them into practical applications within the music is difficult to explain. Some critics profess that a conductor must be born with these abilities while others say they can be taught.

During an interview by Bernard Jacobson with James Levine, Music Director of the New York Metropolitan Opera and Boston Symphony, Levine sheds light on this subject. He expresses the ability to look beyond a composer's intentions and explains how he thinks about music and what he does to prepare for a performance in *Conductors on Conducting* (Columbia Publishing Company, Frenchtown, NJ):

Let's take something we both know from a certain standpoint. You go and you hear a Mozart performance, and here comes a performance in which the tempos have just the right amount of forward motion, but they are poised. The string sound is luminous and radiant but precise and clear and it crackles, but when it's precise and clear and it crackles it doesn't sound shut down and pinpointed and tight, and when it's let to sing out it doesn't get out all floppy and lose its tensility. And when the winds play, it sounds fresh and it sounds open, and you can hear all the notes individually but you can also hear them as a chord, and each telling little thing that happens in the orchestration that's like a new horizon happens and it's full of wonder.

And now comes another performance where the tempos are—they're not wrong, you can't say they're wrong, and you can't say they were not playing together, and you can't say the sound was ugly, none of that. And yet the rhythm has no buoyancy, the sound is a little drab, the winds come in and it lacks luminosity, it lacks radiance, it lacks transparency, it lacks glow. It doesn't smile. What an asinine thing to try to say! But, nonetheless, it's true, and when you have that experience, you experience it as a loss of style, do you not? An absence or a lack of style.

David Ewen also has an interesting point of view about a conductor's qualification in *The Man with the Baton* (Thomas Y. Crowell Company, NY):

Why, of all the branches of musical art, have we had no precocious orchestral conductors to impress us with performances as deeply as so many prodigies of the violin and piano have done? The answer should be apparent. Conducting, unlike composition or the playing of any instrument, demands not merely a native talent for musical expression, but a broad and thorough musical education, an integration of personality. It is a subtle and complicated art that can be mastered only—even with all the talent in the world—after arduous training and intensive study.

Josef Krips, the first music director for whom I worked, was emotionally connected to the music. As a young musician, right out of school, it was inspiring to experience such passion from a conductor. I'll never forget his many performances of *Don Juan* by Richard Strauss—one of his favorites. He lived the story while on the podium and like many conductors who do not simply beat time, he became excited when the music approached a climax (with its increasing dynamics and slowing tempo). Conductors, like Krips, tend to hold back the downbeat to emphasize a decisive moment in the score and their conducting patterns sometimes become a bit difficult to follow. Percussionists usually play on the downbeat of climatic measures with a cymbal crash or a powerful stroke on the bass drum and they must wait until the last possible micro second to avoid an early entrance. That's where the saying originates: "The first one in loses." I eventually learned to watch the concertmaster—when his bow began the downbeat, I played.

The story of *Don Juan* ends with his death. The final notes represent the protagonist's heartbeat and the very last note signifies his demise. As the audience applauded (many times with standing ovations), Krips, so engrossed with the story line, was unable to move or acknowledge the applause. The orchestra, also frozen in place, stared at him in silence. After leaving the stage with slow robotic steps, he finally returned to make a slight gesture of a bow and with a wave of his hand, motioned the orchestra to stand. As for me, it was exciting to experience such emotion from a conductor.

Maestro Krips was well versed in the standard classical repertoire, but not comfortable conducting contemporary music (as were many conductors of that era). At times, however, 5/8 measures (that have only five beats) contained six beats because Krips took a slight pause after the fifth beat—1, 2, 3, 4, 5, pause.

I must admit I have had my preferences among the five music directors with whom I worked, and I sincerely appreciated Krips commitment to the music and his non-wavering passion. He accomplished his goals by having the orchestra play through the music until we got it right. Then, Krips would say: "Just a few measures from the *beginn*" (German for beginning), and, once again, conduct through the entire work!

After his retirement from the San Francisco Symphony, Seiji Ozawa took the orchestra on a European tour. Krips (who lived in Vienna) gave a party for musicians in his hometown of Grinzing. Laurie McGaw (Associate Principal Trumpet) shares this story:

Josef Krips, the previous Music Director of the SFS gave the orchestra a party in Grinzing, a district in the northwest of Vienna. This beautiful area is home to many vineyards and has been the inspiration for the likes of Schubert and Beethoven. The graves of von Doderer, Mahler and other famous Austrians are there. At one of the typical wine restaurants, we were served some of the local wines and foods. Maestro Krips visited each table to give a greeting to his old friends. At our table, one of the trumpet players asked Krips to "tell us something about Grinzing." His response was typical of him: "Ah, Grinzing; that is the place in Vienna where I was born," completely ignoring the world-famous figures who had also lived and died there.

Seiji Ozawa came from the Toronto Symphony to San Francisco as its next music director, still fresh from his days as an Assistant Conductor to Leonard Bernstein at the New York Philharmonic. He brought an entirely different repertoire than Krips' heavily Germanic programs, adding the exciting music of French and Russian composers, as well as a large dose of contemporary music. There is no doubt that Ozawa was a young, talented, exciting, demanding, and charismatic conductor and some of my greatest performance memories come from his tenure with the orchestra. In my opinion, as a music director, however, he was a difficult person with whom to work. Roland Kohloff, Principal Timpanist, was called into his office on several occasions. It was not long after this that the New York Philharmonic posted an opening for Principal Timpani. After hearing the best candidates from around the world and not finding a suitable replacement, the personnel manager called Kohloff to ask if he would consider auditioning for the position. He accepted the invitation, won the job, and the San Francisco Symphony lost one of the finest timpanists in the world. In fact, during Ozawa's tenure, all principal chair players were either demoted, took early retirement, or left the orchestra (with the exception of the principal flute and principal oboe).

Following Ozawa, Edo de Waart, a relatively unknown conductor at the time, joined the San Francisco Symphony as its music director. His rehearsals were very straight-forward and, in my opinion, he did not have much to say about the music. De Waart's rehearsal atmosphere was very casual and musicians responded with such antics as placing a cardboard cow in the seats behind the orchestra when rehearsing the Mahler Symphony No. 6 (that used multiple cowbells).

Herbert Blomstedt, the fourth music director for whom I worked, is a gentleman of the highest caliber and well known as the former Director of the Dresden Staatskapelle in East Germany, one of the oldest orchestras in the world. He brought with him the great

European traditions with a heavy dose of Germanic repertoire. All of the Nielsen symphonies, a composer with whom we had little exposure, were recorded during Blomstedt's time in San Francisco.

Always the consummate professional, he addressed everyone as Mr., Miss, or Mrs., with the greatest respect. Although a taskmaster, to be sure, an orchestra will always rise to the level asked of them.

When it was announced he was to assume the position of our next music director, we were also informed that he was not able to rehearse on Saturday mornings since his religion (Seventh Day Adventist) observes their Sabbath from sundown Friday to sundown Saturday. Whenever Blomstedt conducted, therefore, Saturday rehearsals were moved to Friday mornings. I was pleased with this change because it freed this day to spend with my family. The regular symphony schedule includes four to five concerts a week, including Saturday morning rehearsals and evening performances, with some Sunday matinees. Such a schedule can play havoc with a musician's social life. So, a free Saturday morning was a big deal.

The orchestra wondered how Blomstedt was able to conduct Friday night concerts and still adhere to his religious obligations. According to management, rehearsals were considered work and not allowed on the Sabbath, but performances were comparable to preaching sermons and were permitted on the Sabbath.

It is a tradition for music directors to host a party for symphony personnel after the final concert of a tour. Blomstedt,

*is the ideal ensemble spirit and they are the surpass-
ing stylists of the music world.*

My orchestral career came to an end under the baton of Michael Tilson Thomas. He had been a frequent guest conductor with the San Francisco Symphony for more than twenty years before assuming the title of music director. MTT (as he is affectionately known) brought a refreshing and dynamic change to the orchestra, quite different from Blomstedt's thoughtful and highly-structured approach. Michael has a large and varied repertoire and, never the purist, takes a "no-holds-barred" attitude while on the podium. His interpretations are enhanced by a fantastic imagination for phrasing, dynamics, articulation, and passion. As music director, there was never any doubt about his desire to exploit the amazing potential of a symphony orchestra. One of his greatest contributions to the San Francisco Symphony was to restore contemporary repertoire to heights rarely achieved by his predecessors or peers. MTT carefully chooses scores and, with total commitment to his goals, returned *avant-garde* music to the subscription series. Not simply satisfied to share his passion for music through a performance, Michael begins each concert that contains a new work with a well-crafted discourse about the composition and composer. He has everyone loving the piece before the first note is played.

Another great addition by Michael to San Francisco Symphony programs is his contribution to Music Festivals. Although the orchestra had performed festivals in the past, they were not produced to the extent and variety he brought to this venue. His American Mavericks Festival (June, 2000) featured the works of radical American composers and was an absolute stroke of genius.

According to Lukas Foss, well-known composer, conductor, and educator:

> *All artists have to be mavericks and follow their own paths; they have to be obstinate, and have faith in the impossible, which is the creative process* (American Mavericks, University of California Press).

Regarding the *Mavericks festival*, MTT had this to say:

> *The American Mavericks festival was an occasion to re-experience the range and depth of some of the originally inventive and iconoclastic works that perhaps best witness the profound and zany diversity of the United States* (American Mavericks, University of California Press).

Composers represented in this three-week series of concerts were: Charles Ives, John Cage, Morton Feldman, Milton Babbitt, Terry Riley, Carl Ruggles, Crawford Seeger, Meredith Monk, Lukas Foss, Duke Ellington, George Antheil, Lou Harrison, Henry Cowell, David Del Tredici, Edgard Varèse, Steve Reich, Earle Brown, Steven Mackey, Frank Zappa, Conlon Nancarrow, John Adams, and Aaron Copland. Through courage and foresight, these true mavericks of contemporary music changed the direction of musical thought.

An additional passion of MTT is the works of Gustav Mahler. Not that performing Mahler was anything new to symphony orchestras, but Michael brought these masterpieces to another level. Besides holding Mahler Festivals, the orchestra recorded all nine of his symphonies, including the *Adagio* from Symphony No. 10 (*Unfinished*), along with most of Mahler's vocal works with orchestra. There were also the Russian Festivals, dealing with the revolution and its suffering for the Motherland. These composers expressed it all: rage, fury, zeal, anger, grief, misery, depression, desolation, and gloom. And with fervent passion, Michael wrung every drop of blood from the score!

Never at a loss for words, he spends quite a bit of time on the podium clearly explaining his intentions to the orchestra. At times, he sings out in the outrageous style of James Brown (and in the spirit of Arturo Toscanini) to obtain a special moment in the music. Not satisfied with the limitations of the English language, Michael continues to create his own terminology to extract the passion intended for the moment. The following is a collection of "MTT Speak" that my percussion colleagues and I have collected over the years:

obliterato	Louder than possible
molto obliterato	A percussionist's favorite dynamic
noble forte	Loud with nobility. (You'll know if it's not)
burbalando	In a bubbly manner

dandelion music	Puff, puff (as if blowing on a flowering dandelion)
Vince DeRosa crescendo	A rich, thick, creamy, dark *crescendo*
natürlich Bambi world	Pastoral
offish	As when string players lift the bow off the string
kind of flowing with the sound	We have not been able to exactly define this one
gushalando	"Schmaltzy," like show business
stretchalando	Rubber like
staccatissimo fuss budget	Defies definition
surgealando	In a surging manner
schlepalando	The opposite of *nicht schleppen* (do not drag)
tempo de fight song	Go Niners!

Michael also adds an extra measure of articulation to a score, for example, when composers indicate wedge-shaped accents (stronger than normal accents), he yells out while conducting: "More wedgies, more wedgies!"

MTT is the epitome of a conductor in search of an interpretation. The images that emanate from his words, the movement of his body and baton, and his dynamic level of communication and interaction with the orchestra, all contribute to his desire to create a unique and distinct musical experience.

When does a conductor go too far and how true should one be to a composer's directions? What is blasphemous, and who can claim to possess the ultimate interpretation of any musical work? Unquestionably, not any one conductor and, certainly, no music critic! A conductor can be a composer's best friend or worst enemy but, as an orchestral musician, I am thankful for those who "push the envelope." I will always choose excitement over purity and perfection.

Daniel Barenboim, pianist, conductor and, most recently, Music Director of the Chicago Symphony, expresses his philosophy in the chapter, *On Interpretation*, from his biography: *A Life in Music* (MacMillan Publishing Company, NY):

> *If the score says allegro, and you play adagio, then you have gone too far; similarly if the score says 'crescendo' and you play 'diminuendo.' Freedom of rhythm should neither occur willfully nor capriciously. All these elements must, in some way, relate to the organic whole. There are, of course, stylistic differences between composers: some things, especially as regards volume and flexibility of tempo, are possible for Puccini but certainly wrong for Bach, or viceversa. But the concept of freedom is the same for Bach, Stravinsky, Puccini or Wagner. I do not attempt to change the composer's instructions. But I try to find a relationship between the different instructions. This relationship also applies to the quantity: when it says*

accelerando—how much? and when it says diminu-
endo—how much? And when it says nothing . . . ?

Another example of how a conductor expresses passion from the podium comes from a quote about one of the most celebrated conductors of our time, Arturo Toscanini, in David Ewen's, *The Man with the Baton* (Thomas Y. Crowell Company, NY):

> *Usually, Toscanini tries to explain his conception of phrasing and color by singing the music at the top of his high-pitched, sharp, cracked voice. Sometimes he will hurl unrelated adjectives at the players, adjectives which are supposed to epitomize the mood of the score. He characterizes each sound. One chord is described by him as a "fist;" a staccato note is said to be "mischievous;" this phrase must depict hate, another lust.*
>
> *But when words and song and epigram fail him in his attempt to depict his subtle conceptions (and very frequently they do), Toscanini will then dance and posture and act—try almost any antic that occurs to him at the moment—in order to bring his meaning forcefully to the consciousness of the players.*

Even the audition process took on another level of perfection under Michael's direction. Never one to make rash judgments, there were a few auditions that ended with no decisions. If there were one or two top candidates, he occasionally had them perform with the orchestra for several weeks (instead of the usual one or two

weeks) before selecting a finalist. His search for excellence continues to touch every aspect of orchestral life and although he can be
demanding and relentless in his pursuit of virtuosity, I found him
to be fair and a person who treats orchestra members with respect.

An enlightening remark about the nature of a conductor is
found in Richard Osborne's book, regarding the famous conductor, Herbert von Karajan, in *Herbert von Karajan: A life in Music*.
Osborne quotes a postscript to a letter written in Vienna on January
28, 1950, by Walter Legge, founder of the London Philharmonia
(Excerpt by Richard Osborne from *Herbert Von Karajan: A Life in Music [Copyright*
© *Richard Osborne, 1998]* is reproduced by permission of PFD (www.PFD.co.uk)
on behalf of Richard Osborne):

> *There is no form of occupation which has a worse
> effect on a man's character than that of a conductor.
> In the practice of it a man has for six hours a day, five
> days or six days a week, undisputed and dictatorial
> powers over a large body of experts in his own field
> and thinking. He has frequently similar powers over
> the most eminent soloists, instrumentalists, and sing-
> ers. When it comes to a performance, it is he who culls
> the praise and the applause, not only for the orches-
> tra's work, but for the creations of men whose boots he
> is, in the main, not fit to lick. Is it a wonder that the
> exercise of these dictatorial powers and the reaping
> of other men's harvests makes conductors impatient
> in normal relationships of the slightest opposition to
> their will?*

It seems that when too much power is given to any one individual, the result is not always amiable. And, with music directors, when their responsibilities cross over from musical to personnel decisions, the potential for controversy is always present.

Strict contract rules make it impossible for music directors to fire a member of the orchestra at will, but with constant intimidation and reseating, some players resign or take early retirement. Orchestral musicians can only take so much pressure from a conductor before it interferes with their ability to perform at the high professional level required of them.

Isn't it astounding that well-educated, highly-trained, professional orchestral musicians, outstanding singers, pianists, and instrumental soloists concede so much of their musical opinions to conductors. Yet, this is how a symphony orchestra operates. If players were to vote on how loud, soft, fast, slow, or any of the hundreds of other musical directives that could apply to a measure of music, no decision would be unanimous. Still, as members of a major orchestra, would we have it any other way? Probably not. And would the opinions of one hundred musicians produce a more musical result than that of one conductor? I doubt it. So, it is the music director and guest conductors who take responsibility for, and reap the benefit of, the efforts of musicians, soloists, and composers whose contributions comprise *The Great American Symphony Orchestra.*

COMMITTEES: THE MAJORITY RULES

A committee is a group of people who individually can do nothing, but who, as a group, can meet and decide that nothing can be done.

—Fred Allen

Members of a symphony orchestra govern themselves and maintain a relationship with management through its various committees by electing colleagues to conduct non-musical activities during the symphony season. Since these committees have direct contact with administration, orchestra members select peers who possess political, managerial, confrontational, perceptive, diplomatic, and (most importantly) common-sense skills.

The Players' Committee provides a direct liaison to the personnel manager in order to handle pertinent orchestra business. This committee addresses grievances, contract disputes, last-minute requests for schedule changes, and inquiries from orchestra personnel. The players' committee is quite active and can be called to assemble at a moment's notice for urgent matters during rehearsals or concert intermissions. When a vote is required, the full orchestra must be convened.

The committee elects one member as the Chair who becomes the "go-to" person, facilitating queries between management and orchestra members, and attends a yearly Board of Director's meeting to report on pertinent orchestra business. I served as chair of the player's committee several times. When I presented my first report, hoping to create a rapport with Board members, I opened the presentation by telling them how different sections of an orchestra could be compared to sport teams:

> *The string section is like a basketball team; they constantly run up and down the court, playing thousands of notes, rarely stopping for a rest. The brass and woodwind sections are like a football team; they come out of the huddle, make a magnificent entrance with loud dynamics and piercing melodic lines. Then, they wait on the sidelines for their next appearance. The percussion section can be compared to a baseball team because they sit in the dugout a lot! Occasionally, they come up to the plate, hit a home run with a deafening sound on the gong or cymbals or a thunderous roar on the timpani or bass drum. Once again, they return to the dugout.*

They laughed, I relaxed, and we got down to business.

The chair's job is quite a task. Besides daily interactions with musicians and management, this person acts as head of the *Complaint Department*, creates agendas for meetings, and confers with other committees. The chair is also responsible for selecting five of the ten orchestra members that serve on the audition committee (management chooses the other five representatives). The chair's main responsibility, however, is to conduct orchestra meetings (managed by Robert's Rules of Order). It's quite a challenge to maintain order for more than one hundred musicians, especially when contentious issues arise. Members use this time to influence other musicians who have not yet decided how to vote on a particular matter. Robert's Rules of Order is designed to allow meetings to proceed in a fair and controlled manner; consequently, it's important the chair has a good working knowledge of the rules because there are always those who enjoy "getting on a soap box" and have trouble limiting their remarks. Unless the chair sets a maximum time limit for each speaker, a "call for the question" has to be requested which requires a vote to end the discussion or to allow it to continue.

Although the chair leads the meeting, this person may not interject an opinion while acting in this capacity. If he or she wants to make a statement regarding an issue, the chair must temporarily step down from the podium to address members. A committee secretary is present at all meetings and maintains a list of players who wish to speak.

Most meetings run smoothly but there are times, such as during a work stoppage (when an orchestra is on strike), that discussions can become heated with emotions running wild. A decision to continue to strike until work-related issues can be resolved is never unanimous and the fact that members are not receiving paychecks, definitely adds to the stress. But, as with any democratic organization, the majority rules, and musicians continue to negotiate until they are satisfied with the contract and a vote is taken to accept management's proposal.

The Negotiating Committee, in my opinion, is the most important body that represents an orchestra. Since the union does not negotiate for players, this committee is the official collective-bargaining representative of the American Federation of Musicians Union. It only meets during a contract-renewal year for the sole purpose of hammering out a new contract. This committee spends countless hours in meetings (with or without the orchestra), discussing issues that need to be addressed for the upcoming contract. They literally spend days and nights meeting with the management team and deliberate on all areas of the agreement: scheduling, touring, benefits, pension, auditions, vacation, sick leave, sabbaticals, leaves of absence, and compensation. The subject of compensation, alone, is quite a complex issue since it includes:

- Payments and fees for the audition committee
- Disability insurance
- Doubling (players who perform on instruments not specified in their contract, for example, a clarinetist who plays the bass clarinet or saxophone)
- Extra services (beyond contract limits)
- Long-term sick leave
- Other types of leaves (personal or emergency)
- Tour fees (additional salary when touring)
- Tour per diem (added compensation for food and miscellaneous expenses)
- Personal weekly salary (base salary plus negotiated overscale)
- Radio broadcast fees
- Run-out fees (travel outside the area with no overnight stay)
- Sabbaticals (three and six months)

- Seniority pay (extra pay based on years of service)
- Sick leave
- Extra-player (substitute) compensation
- Audio Exploitation fee (radio and internet broadcasts)

This type of committee-administration interaction is rarely found in the traditional workplace, that is, employees who negotiate directly with management regarding working conditions, compensation, and benefits. Although a union representative is always present during negotiations, orchestra members do the actual work. Technically, the contract is with the American Federation of Musicians, however, union officials do not have the necessary or detailed knowledge of an orchestra's working environment or artistic needs so the negotiating committee becomes the legal bargaining agent.

Contract negotiations with the San Francisco Symphony were confrontational for many years, with both sides (musicians and management) coming to the table with a long list of demands. The atmosphere was very intense as one side tried to persuade the other regarding the benefits of their particular terms and conditions. New contracts invariably included refining existing language as well as adding additional provisions to resolve controversial issues. More times than not, meetings went past contract deadlines, requiring the orchestra to take a vote to play and talk under the old agreement or to strike. It was rare for any major compromises to take place if orchestra members continued to work; consequently, a strike of one or two weeks, sanctioned by the American Federation

Labor Union, was necessary before a settlement could be reached. The two longest strikes that occurred during my tenure with the San Francisco Symphony were for seven and nine weeks.

Although losing a paycheck for such a long period of time was difficult, the resulting contracts brought many gains and elevated the Symphony to one of the top ten orchestras in the United States (with regard to salary and benefits).

Several meetings took place during the 1973 seven-week strike and musicians were quite unhappy with management and the Music Director, Josef Krips, for extending it for such a long period of time. Since this was considered a lock-out (management refused to allow musicians to go back to work without a contract), orchestra members were able to receive unemployment compensation. When I applied, I was asked if I had any other income. I said: "Yes, I make $125 a month as a part-time employee at San Jose State University." The response I got was that I was not eligible for unemployment compensation since I had other income. I replied: "But, I have a family and can't afford to live on $125 a month." They said: "When you're on strike, you're not supposed to live—you're just supposed to exist!"

During Krips' tenure, he established a system of co-principal first-chair players (which was never popular with the orchestra). He would decide which co-principal would play the major work on the program (usually a symphony), leaving the other co-principal with the responsibility of performing the overture and concerto (as an example). It wasn't long before co-principals realized there was an **A** and a **B** team. This ranking system eventually permeated the air and all musicians began to see themselves either in the maestro's favor (**A** team) or out of his favor (**B** team). At one of the more contentious orchestra meetings on this subject, a disgruntled member said: "I'd like to speak for the **C** team," bringing a bit of levity to a very tense situation.

Years later, the San Francisco Symphony received a $100 thousand grant from the Hewlett Packard Foundation to obtain the services of a professional management team led by Robert H. Mnookin, Professor of Law at Harvard Law School and Chair of the Steering Committee of Harvard's Program on Negotiation. Since he had developed a Conflict Resolution Program, the grant enabled the Symphony to invite him and his team to San Francisco to present workshops and training sessions for management and orchestra members. The meetings included ideas to:

- Create a more positive and satisfying working environment for both musicians and management
- Improve working relationships at the negotiation table
- Increase effective communication
- Demonstrate an understanding of everyone's interests, concerns, and goals
- Develop negotiation skills
- Improve the capacity for better managing tension between musicians and administration

- Approach negotiations in a problem-solving way
- Document how other orchestras and non-profit organizations manage labor negotiations

To put it simply, instead of coming to the table with a "laundry list" of demands, both sides came with a new attitude: *What can we do to help you with your concerns?* An amazing difference was felt in the negotiation process and for the first time, a six-year agreement was signed. This was only the second time in the Symphony's history that a contract was negotiated without a work stoppage. Previous contracts had lasted only three years. But, in retrospect, such a long contract caused orchestra members to lose ground with regard to salary and benefits when compared to other major American orchestras because the negotiating committee underestimated projections in wages that would have occurred. As a new executive director and changes in orchestra personnel took place, negotiations were no longer based on conflict resolution or interest-based bargaining but returned to the mutual positional strategies of the past. Both sides, once again, came to the table with pre-set conditions, hoping to trade to reach their goals.

Other orchestra committees include: Musical Advisory, Tour, Audition, Review, Health, Retirement Board, Non-Renewal, and Reseating.

The Musical Advisory Committee only serves in an informational capacity and occasionally meets with the music director and other administrative personnel to discuss artistic matters that affect the orchestra, for example, concert repertoire and guest conductors. It also shares ideas regarding day-to-day and long-term musical matters.

Management is generally wary of giving orchestra members too much power or influence over a music director since the position comes with full authority for musical decisions. Stanley Leonard, long-time member of the Pittsburgh Symphony, shares management's advice to committee members regarding their Artistic Committee:

> *When the Artistic Committee of the Pittsburgh Symphony Orchestra was organized, I was its Chairman. We were given explicit directions about what the Music Director's contract said about his control over artistic matters and we were to be careful not to step on his prerogatives. When we had our first meetings, the Music Director solicited ideas from us. Touché!*

The Tour Committee convenes when an upcoming tour schedule is announced to study the itinerary and confirm that all current contract provisions have been met, for example, number of concerts and rehearsals, travel arrangements, hotel accommodations, proper amount of acoustic rehearsals, per-diem expenses, daily hours of travel, free days, and transportation of personnel from hotels to concert halls. If management requests a deviation from the contract while on tour, this committee advises orchestra members who then must vote on the issue.

The Audition Committee meets when an opening occurs within the orchestra. This is the only committee to receive remuneration for their service since the audition process takes so much time outside of normal working hours.

The San Francisco Symphony has two Review Committees, one for strings and another for brass, woodwinds, and percussion. These committees vote on candidates who have won an audition and are performing with the orchestra as probationary members. At the end of the first season (audition year), the review committee and music director vote as to whether a player will be asked to remain for another season (probationary year). At the end of the probationary year, a second vote is taken to determine whether or not the player will be hired as a tenured orchestra member. If both the orchestra committee and music director cast "yes" votes, the candidate is offered a tenured contract.

The Retirement Board is one of only two committees (Health) that include representation from both management and the orchestra (four each). The retirement board manages the retirement plan (although changes must first be approved by the Board of Governors). Orchestras that provide pension funds for employees operate under rules established by ERISA (Employee Retirement Income Security Act), a federal agency that oversees private pension plans.

The Health Committee is jointly staffed by management and orchestra personnel. Their only function is to review the orchestra's health plan, annual costs, and to educate musicians on health-related policy changes made by the insurance carrier (coverage, co-payments, or prescription drug costs).

A musician must have thirty years of service in an orchestra and be at least sixty-two years of age to qualify for a full pension. There is also the *Rule of 85* that states a member can retire with full benefits if his or her years of service, plus age, equals or exceeds 85 years—the player, however, must be at least sixty years old to qualify.

In the past, some symphony orchestras chose not to provide private pension plans, opting instead to join the American Federation of Musicians Union Pension Plan. In this case, management contributed a percentage of each player's salary directly to the union fund. This is no longer an attractive option since unions are now facing financial problems. A symphony's private pension plan is part of the bargaining agreement and not based on a percentage of a player's salary; therefore, during negotiations, management can offer players a total pay package which gives them an opportunity to split the money between salary, pension, and benefits.

The Non-Renewal Committee convenes when a music director decides to fire a tenured member of an orchestra. The only cause for non-renewal of contract for artistic matters is: *Material deficiency in musical performance and material failure to perform at the artistic level of the Orchestra* . . . . Since it is extremely difficult to prove a player is not performing up to orchestral standards, the non-renewal committee rarely meets. It is more likely that a music director will attempt to demote a musician to another chair within the section. A wind player, for instance, could be moved from the assistant principal position to the second or third chair or a string player reseated to the back of the section. Orchestra members, however, have the right to appeal any decision through the reseating committee. There is also another clause in the contract that deals with *Dismissal for Cause,* that is, insubordination.

The Reseating Committee convenes when an orchestra member has been advised that a music director intends to reseat a player and the musician wants to appeal the decision. Once again, the sole cause for reseating a player is that their performance is below the standard required for the position. Unfortunately, a musician's motor skills can deteriorate over a lifetime of continual repetitive motions; some players recognize this and grudgingly agree to move to a less-demanding chair. For others, it's a matter of pride, and they're not always willing to be demoted. A real heartache occurs when musicians approach retirement age and a music director does not allow them to complete their remaining years in the seats they, most likely, held during their entire careers. What's important to remember, though, is that whatever a musician may lose in motor skills is compensated for by their years of experience.

Other than agreed-upon voting procedures, most committees function in an advisory capacity with no "teeth." In other words, musicians can complain (bark) but they have no power (bite)

to change management's viewpoint. Any disagreements regarding existing contractual procedures between orchestra personnel and administration must be handled through the Grievance and Arbitration procedures as outline in the contract. If management brings a one-time request to the player's committee for something not provided for in the contract, the orchestra meets to vote on the issue. If the orchestra brings a non-contractual request to management, they take it under advisement and either approve or deny it. Each side has the prerogative to agree or disagree on matters not covered in the contract. During full orchestra meetings, motions are passed with a majority of "aye" votes, except for money issues that take a two-thirds majority to pass.

All committees research, organize, document, and clarify agenda items before presenting them to musicians for a vote. Then, the majority rules! First, a voice vote is taken; if it is not conclusive, a hand count is required. If there is a contentious motion, voting takes place by secret ballot. Any orchestra member can request a secret ballot during a meeting.

The organization of committees within an orchestra provides direct involvement between workers and management (which is almost unheard of in the business world). Because there was abuse and disregard for the needs of musicians by music directors and administrators during the early organization of symphony orchestras, players began to demand equal say in matters that affected them. It has only been during the last sixty years that orchestra members have insisted on contractual procedures to protect their rights.

To reiterate, in a modern orchestra, committees operate as a democracy even though a music director rules as a dictator.

THE GOOD & THE BAD

Nothing is better than music . . . It has done more for us than we have the right to hope for.

—Nadia Boulanger

Whenever I'm asked what I do for a living, I say: "I'm a member of the San Francisco Symphony." The usual response is: "How lucky you are to have a career doing something you love." This is certainly true and comes under the heading of *The Good* for this chapter. Yet, what one considers good or bad is strictly a matter of opinion.

To have studied and performed the greatest music ever written from the 18th to 21st Centuries is certainly at the top of my list. Sitting next to so many outstanding musicians, in front of sold-out concerts, and playing under the world's celebrated conductors has been, for me, beyond my wildest dreams. I find it astounding to think of the hundreds of compositions I have played by such great composers as Mahler, Strauss, Stravinsky, Copland, Bartók, Debussy, Shostakovich, Prokofiev—the list is endless. And, as a composer myself, I never cease to be amazed by the genius of these men to produce drama, excitement, love, sadness, euphoria, melancholy, passion, majesty, anger, death, spirit, warmth, humor, tranquility, grief, elegance, pain, fury, joy, fear, peace, serenity, rage, laughter, gloom, mystery, grace, hopelessness, and vigor from a musical score. Moments I consider to be the most exceptional are: The Tone Poems of Richard Strauss, *Symphonie Fantastique* by Hector Berlioz, the beautiful melodies of Gustav Mahler (especially his *Adagietto* from Symphony No. 5), Beethoven's Symphony No. 9, and Claude Debussy's *La Mer*. And, I never tire of hearing the repeated performances of Igor Stravinsky's *The Rite of Spring*. One of my continuing goals as a composer is to write a successful fugue (which still eludes me—even though I've heard so many great ones).

I had an epiphany during a Literature and Materials Class (music theory) while a student at The Juilliard School. It was then I realized I could be a composer. We were asked to write short compositions in various styles and even though I enjoyed the assignments, I never thought of myself as a composer; that is, until my fourth year of study with Vincent Persichetti. He made a statement that stuck with me my entire life (quoted on Page 120). What he said convinced me that I, too, could write music. When I say I am a composer, I use the term loosely, even though I did win a Special Distinction Award from the ASCAP Rudolph Nissim Composition Contest in 1999 for my orchestral work enti-tled: *Pentadic Striations*.

While on the subject of compositions, I'd like to share a musical ditty, a play on words, about *Carmina Burana* by Carl Orff. It's set to the famous melody, *Let's Call the Whole Thing Off* by George Gershwin (1937 film: *Shall We Dance*).

Read the words carefully:

When considering *The Bad* about a career in a symphony orchestra, the first thing that comes to mind is having to perform under the baton of a music director who does not resonate with one's musical tastes. His or her choice of repertoire, rehearsal techniques, conducting skills, lack of musicianship, and individual personality traits can all contribute to an unhappy musician. It is especially disturbing to players when unprofessional conductors glance at a performer or an entire section when a mistake is made. This type of gesture is not only distracting but disturbs an orchestra's concentration—not to mention the resentment generated towards that particular conductor. Charles Blackman discusses this problem with particular insight in *Behind the Baton* (Charos Enterprises, Inc., NY):

> *Many conductors feel it is necessary to exaggerate their reaction to every error in order to prove they are astute, know the score thoroughly and hear everything. Quite often, we find one who thinks it necessary to let the players know "they cannot fool him," or "get away with anything." It is particularly interesting, for, almost without exception, no orchestral player really tries to "fool" the conductor or "get*

away with anything." His own pride and training assure his best efforts. Also, it is very rare that the orchestra does not hear and recognize a mistake at the same time. In fact, they know the cause before the conductor becomes aware of it. What, then, is accomplished when a conductor directs at a player what is called "a dirty look," or claps his hand to his head in despair, or pulls one ear lobe? Even, as I have seen at one performance, pretend to stab himself with the baton!

It's interesting to note the differences between the talent necessary to conduct and the talent required to compose. Although both professions include a tremendous amount of formal study and a high degree of innate ability, there is one obvious distinction between the two crafts—that is, personality. Composing is done in the solitude of a studio and does not demand an exuberant persona in order to communicate a sense of passion in the music. Conducting, however, requires an ability to communicate expressive qualities from a score to musicians and the audience. It is important, therefore, that a conductor possess a captivating personality, a singing voice, fluid arm and body movements, appropriate facial expressions, and a command of the English language (for American orchestras).

Not all successful conductors have an overtly outward charismatic presence on the podium and, in fact, some are very reserved. Three conductors come to mind who exhibit a remark-able sense of musicality and have the ability to convey their inten-tions to an orchestra with a minimum amount of motion: Fritz Reiner, George Szell, and Vladimir Ashkenazy. Their attention to detail, intonation, and an intense commitment to a composer's directives can be felt by musicians who, in turn, respond accord-ingly. An audience, however, may not be able to see or recognize these subtle nuances, and without a more visual communication from the conductor, a sense of the character, emotion, and musical energy in the score can be lost. I believe it is also important for the audience to have a visual component since a great deal of their time is spent looking at the conductor. The eye captures and trans-mits the conductor's movements and gestures to the brain while the ear delivers the sound.

Since this dichotomy exists between conductors and compos-ers, it's not unusual that when a composer conducts his or her own music, it is rarely inspirational. Exceptions to this rule can be found in such artists as Leonard Bernstein (former Music Director of the New York Philharmonic), Esa-Pekka Salonen (Principal Conductor and Artistic Advisor of the Philharmonia Orchestra in London and Conductor Laureate of the Los Angeles Philharmonic), and Gustav Mahler (who had a successful career in Europe as a Symphonic and Operatic conductor). But, it's more likely for great composers to dis-tinguish themselves as great conductors than the reverse.

G. Révész looks at this question from a psychological perspec-tive, implying there are two types of talent, one for conducting and another for composing in *The Psychology of Music* (Harcourt and Brace, NY):

In music we must differentiate two types of talent; namely, the creative and the reproductive-interpretative. The later is sub-divided into instrumental-virtuoso talent and talent for conducting.

Although the creative and the reproductive-interpretative talents are sometimes combined in one person, they still represent two highly independent, and by nature, altogether distinct, types of talent. This is shown in the fact that the two do not usually go together. None of the great organists, pianists, violinists, and conductors, with few exceptions, were distinguished composers. Even though they often engaged in creative work, they nevertheless very rarely succeeded in producing works of high value in a musical sense. Their compositions lack originality, show the influence of great composers, and knuckle to current taste.

Eminent instrumentalists find it difficult to produce anything outstanding, for the simple reason that a virtuoso performance on any instrument demands such a great subordination, such an inward absorption in a composition not one's own, such a degree of self control, and such specialized technical training, that there is scarcely any energy left for the development of a creative gift.

One of the most memorable moments of my career occurred when I was still young, impressionable, and fresh out of The Juilliard School. Igor Stravinsky had been invited to guest conduct the San Francisco Symphony and came with his associate, Robert Kraft (who actually directed the difficult works on the program, including *The Rite of Spring*). Stravinsky conducted one work, not only because he was old, but he didn't have a refined baton technique.

Nevertheless, he certainly had great enthusiasm for the music and his reputation as a composer superseded any lack of technique he had as a conductor. He was a great inspiration to all the musicians.

Occasionally, there are incidences that have a humbling effect on conductors. One year, an up-and-coming, dynamic, and exciting Russian Maestro, Valery Gergiev, guest conducted the Symphony. He wore a white vest under his black tailcoat that became detached (at the back) during the performance, causing the two ends to dangle beneath his jacket. The audience's attention was now focused on the unattached vest as the tails swayed back and forth to the rhythm of the music. When he realized what had happened, Gergiev frantically tried to pick up the loose ends with his left hand while continuing to conduct with his right hand. He attempted to shove the ends of the vest into the inside pockets of the jacket—but to no avail. This continued for most of the work and the orchestra could hardly keep from laughing. To his credit, Gergiev finished the piece; but, when he returned for the second work, the white vest was nowhere to be seen! To my knowledge, on his many return engagements, he wore a cummerbund.

There are many humbling situations that instrumentalists encounter during performances. Lenore Hatfield, Executive Director and Concertmaster of the Camerata Orchestra in Bloomington, Indiana, and a former member of the Cincinnati

Symphony Orchestra, relates a funny story about a rehearsal of *Symphonie Fantastique* by Hector Berlioz when she was a member of the Indianapolis Symphony:

> *The percussionist, playing this famous bell part [G and C] on a set of chimes, inadvertently struck a wrong note during a rehearsal. This part must be played very loudly; so, in his exuberance he missed the correct note. As a solution, all of the chimes were removed from the rack except the G and C. Wouldn't you know, during the concert, as he went to strike one of the notes, he missed the chime completely and his mallet went through the space between the two notes!*

This famous bell part, usually performed backstage while watching a video monitor, has been the downfall of many percussionists. Stanley Leonard of the Pittsburg Symphony Orchestra relates this story:

> *On one of our concerts at the Proms in London at Royal Festival Hall, we performed Berlioz Symphonie Fantastique. It was televised and later broadcast. We were able to watch, and when the church bell entrance came up in the final movement, the camera zoomed in on the bell and the hammer in the player's hand. The percussionist who was performing this part, missed hitting the bell on the first soft entrance—now seen and not heard by all the world, but before that known to only a few!*

Other examples of what one might consider *The Bad* about a career in a symphony orchestra are night and weekend performances (leaving little time for family and social life), rehearsal schedules that require two trips to the concert hall (10:00 a.m. to 12:30 p.m. rehearsals and 8:00 p.m. to 10:30 p.m. performances, two or three times a week), run-out concerts that require several hours of travel on a bus, and tours from four to six weeks a year. Although tours disrupt family life and teaching commitments, most players enjoy travelling around the world, especially for European audiences where many famous composers were born.

Members of an orchestra rarely choose the city in which they will spend their careers and are considered fortunate to have even won an audition. I certainly could have done much worse than San Francisco! There are musicians who, in order to fulfill their dreams of playing with an orchestra, begin a career outside of the United States—some, never returning home. When I was a student, I was tempted to answer an ad for a percussion opening in the Beirut Lebanon Orchestra, but my wife quickly brought me to my senses.

Life in a symphony orchestra is usually more difficult for our spouses and partners than for the players. When my wife, our six-month old son, and I moved from New York to San Francisco, we left behind family, friends, and familiar surroundings. Leaving the East Coast was much more difficult for Josie than it was for me since I was moving to an exceptional position with an orchestra. At that time, she was a stay-at-home mom and took full responsibility for raising the children, tending to household and financial matters, and had to carve out a new life for herself on the West Coast.

Those who support our careers are not given enough credit for the sacrifices they make. Saul Goodman, a member of the New York Philharmonic from 1926 to 1972, had this to say about his life in an orchestra (Used with permission of the Goodman Estate):

> *On a typical Thursday, I would rehearse until 12:30 p.m. and then teach several students in the basement of Carnegie Hall. With an 8:30 p.m. concert to play, it made little sense to dash home (in the rush hour), throw down my dinner, and return to work.*
>
> *Instead, I would remain in Manhattan, arriving home after the concert around 11:00 at night. By this time, my daughters were asleep. My wife, having to give them dinner, attend to their school needs, and put them to bed, was exhausted. Clearly such a pattern runs counter to family life and generates pressure in many professional musicians' lives.*

In his autobiography, Erich Leinsdorf, former Conductor of the Boston Symphony, defends his attitude regarding a musician's schedule. He laments that after the 1964 Boston Symphony contract negotiations, the committee insisted they would no longer perform on Sunday afternoons. Leinsdorf goes on to say that the committee was following the lead of the New York Philharmonic but pointed out that there were few similarities between the two orchestras. In other words, Boston residents depended primarily on the Boston Symphony for classical musical events whereas New Yorkers did not rely primarily on the New York Philharmonic for symphony concerts. New York is a Mecca for symphonic performances by orchestras from around the world, besides having a plethora of professional chamber and community orchestras in the greater New York area. The following quote is from Leinsdorf's *Cadenza: A Musical Career* (Houghton Mifflin Company, Boston, MA):

> *In my indignation, I made one of my most scathing remarks, and not in camera either: "I expect that the next round of negotiations will rule out all evening concerts to allow our players a more normal home life when the kids are back from school for dinner." I still think that artists should perform when the public has time off to enjoy musical offerings, but evidently the middle-class instincts of the musicians' committee no longer had any feeling for the real mission of players, which is to serve the public.*
>
> *Without being in the least naïve, I have felt all my life that it is a special advantage of the theatrical and musical professions not to be subject to the routine of regular hours, days, and weeks throughout the year. I consider it something out of the ordinary to perform on holidays, when office and shop are shut and when people look to us for recreation, solace and pleasure through great music.*

Without question, security and benefits are a tremendous *Good* about working in a symphony orchestra. Most musicians make a living as freelance players, performing as substitutes for established symphony, opera, and ballet orchestras, as well as musical theater, recording studios, movies, jazz groups, club dates, weddings, jingles, and other gigs. And, although many of these jobs pay well, they do not offer company-paid benefits or tenure. Also, freelance musicians do not have regular work schedules (every day is a work day for them). Their hours range from early-morning rehearsals to late-night recordings or club dates. Michael Colgrass, a well-known American composer, tells a story about his days as a freelance player in New York City in *Adventures of an American Composer* (Copyright © 2010. Used by permission, Meredith Music Publications, MD):

> *I endured a lot of mundane gigs too, like commercials and film soundtracks, but was thankful to be constantly working. Some days I played a rehearsal in the morning, concert in the afternoon, a ballet in the evening, and a recording at midnight. Eventually, I was working so much I almost slept in my dark suit, white shirt, and long face (as the joke went in those days about the overworked freelance musician). But I didn't dare pass up jobs because contractors depended on me to be available. Besides, these gigs were subsidizing my composing.*
>
> *One night, in the midst of my hectic existence, I was carrying my briefcase full of drumsticks and mallets along West 57th Street when I stopped and said, "Am I going to the concert or coming from the concert?" I checked my direction — I was walking west, away from Carnegie Hall, toward the subway, so I had to be heading home!*

Freelance players do not earn vacation pay and many dare not take a holiday for fear of missing a call (gig). The first rule for a working freelance musician is "never turn down an engagement."

The reason is that a contractor will fill the job with another player and, before long, the phone stops ringing. In 1987, George Lucas opened Skywalker Ranch in Marin County, California, and hired local musicians to record his movie sound tracks. I was called for the first session but had to refuse because I was teaching at San Jose State University on that day. I was never called again.

A five-day-a-week schedule, with vacation, benefits, and a weekly pay check is considered a "plum" in the music business. Just the fact that members of an orchestra do not have to transport instruments and equipment to and from freelance venues and are able to store them at the hall, is an added blessing. There is a cut-throat attitude among freelance musicians that once a relationship has been established with a contractor, it must be protected at all costs. Consequently, these players are careful who they recommend for a gig—especially if they are good musicians. Since there is no tenure in the freelance business, if a performer shows up late or falls out of favor with a contractor, he or she may not get another call. This is especially true when other qualified players are available. And, since a musician's motor skills can deteriorate with age, there is always a new crop of young, talented players "waiting in the wings" (like vultures) to gobble up any work. But, as previously mentioned, mature players have the advantage of performing experience over their younger counterparts.

Members of a symphony orchestra also have professional perks, one of which is sign-up jobs. When a concert is programmed that does not fall into the normal contractual schedule, it's offered to orchestra members as a sign-up job. Interested musicians sign the list and any remaining openings are filled by substitute players. One of the more unusual sign-up concerts I played was with the famous Rock Group, *Metallica*. They contracted the Symphony to perform a joint performance at the Berkeley Auditorium.

Approaching the theater for the first rehearsal, I was amazed to see six semitrailer trucks parked in front of the hall. One had been converted to a complete recording studio with, what seemed like, hundreds of cables feeding into the auditorium. The first orchestra session was nothing special and the parts were not difficult. Given the fact that the arranger and conductor was Michael Kamen, a well-known film composer, it didn't surprise me that the orchestra charts sounded like movie music.

I had a very interesting solo for tuned gongs that were mounted on a rack directly behind me and although I spent quite some time practicing this unusual arrangement, the band was so loud that I challenge anyone to say they could hear one note of the solo on the recording.

The stage setup was a wonder in itself. The orchestra took up three fourths of the stage with the band performing directly in front of us. A few crew members were backstage with video cameras attached to long poles, similar to microphones. During the show, these cameras recorded close-ups of *Metallica* and orchestra members which were then displayed on a huge thirty-foot video screen positioned at the rear of the stage for audience viewing.

A bank of approximately fifty amplifiers was placed along one side of the enormous backstage area and, of course, miles of cable were sprawled along the floor, connecting everything together. There were two tables offstage in the wings, each one containing several guitars. I eventually figured out that the guitarists used separate instruments for songs arranged in different keys which allowed them to use the same chord positions with their left hands. During the performance, all they had to do was move offstage and exchange one guitar for another that had been tuned to the new key. We all should be so lucky! I'll bet French horn players wouldn't mind exchanging a horn for a longer or shorter one in a different key so they don't have to transpose. There are, however, a few trumpets and clarinets pitched in different keys (which means a player can use the same fingering, but the pitch will be in a different key).

Metallica put on quite a show and the audience never sat down for the entire two-hour concert. As a percussionist, I was quite taken with Lars Ulrich, *Metallica's* drummer, and his approach to playing drum set. I had never seen a drum set player use such large sticks that allowed him to produce an amazing amount of sound from the drums and cymbals. As I roamed around backstage during rehearsals, I happened to notice a pile of Zildjian cymbals lying on the floor. The fact that they were cracked, smashed, and mutilated should have given me a clue as to what to expect during the performance. Lars destroys several cymbals every night during a concert in order to extract the amount of sound he produces.

The most challenging part of the show was coordinating the orchestra with *Metallica*. During sections of the arrangement, the band took, what we call, *cadenzas* or places in the music where the rhythm stops and the musicians perform free improvised solos. At some point, the orchestra has to make an accurate entrance to, once again, sync up with the Band. This responsibility lies with the conductor, but since Kamen is primarily a composer, he had problems with entrances—but he devised a clever solution, in fact, a very unusual one in our profession. At the next rehearsal, all orchestra musicians were given a set of ear phones for rehearsals and the performance. At first, I thought it was to hear Metallica, sort of like having a monitor (speaker) close by. But, to my surprise, we heard Michael's voice warning us that the band was about to conclude a *cadenza* and that we should get ready for our entrance. No expense was spared for this show and the concert was released as a live recording on DVD, VHS, and CD under the title *S&M* (an acronym for Symphony and *Metallica*).

I had never attended a rock concert before and was very impressed with the entire production. The experience gave me great respect for Rock music as an art. *Metallica* musicians are true artists in their own right and deserve the respect they get from their adoring fans. Performing with this group has even elevated my own status to that of a semi-Rock Star. When I now give a Master Class or meet percussion students at conventions, many of them come up to me (in awe) and say: "Didn't you play with *Metallica*?" I smile, acknowledge my greatness, and give them an autograph!

An orchestral musician's view regarding *The Good* or *The Bad* about a career in a symphony orchestra is strictly a matter of opinion, but the positives surely outweigh any negatives. Unfortunately, there are players who, for any number of reasons, become disillusioned with their position in an orchestra and no longer find joy in the profession. I cannot deny the fact that I was lucky to have had one of the very few percussion positions in a major United States orchestra and the benefit of performing the greatest music ever written—but, I must also credit my teachers and family who coaxed me along and helped to make it all possible.

RULES, RULES, & MORE RULES

*Any tone can succeed any other tone, any tone can sound
simultaneously with any other tone or tones, and any
group of tones can be followed by any other group of tones,
just as any degree of tension or nuance can occur in any
medium under any kind of stress or duration.*

— Vincent Persichetti

There is a set of working conditions in every organization to provide an orderly and efficient method for managing a business, but very few occupations have anything as comprehensive as that of a major symphony orchestra. Orchestras require that all musicians be onstage, at a precise time, in tune, warmed up, and ready to play before a rehearsal or concert can commence. A conductor cannot begin if a wind or percussion player is not present since no one else can play that part. It's not as crucial with the string section because there are multiple first and second violinists, violists, cellists, and bassists who perform the same part. A problem can arise, however, when a string player is absent and a conductor gives the section specific directions regarding a musical passage. If this happens, the musician will not have the benefit of those instructions. For this reason, all players are to be onstage and ready to play before the start of all sessions.

Quite a bit of classical repertoire does not necessitate the services of an entire orchestra. The music of Mozart, for example, calls for a much smaller ensemble than the usual one hundred or so musicians that comprise a major symphony orchestra. Consequently, many string, woodwind, and percussion players are not needed for these rehearsals and concerts. Harp, piano, and percussion are rarely used in much of the standard 19th Century classical repertoire. Beethoven and Brahms symphonies, for example, also use reduced woodwinds and brass (two players in a section instead of three or four) and most of the principal wind chairs have an associate principal to offer them relief from challenging principal parts. Some performers, consequently, are not required to attend rehearsals or concerts in which they do not play.

Although contract regulations require that all players arrive before the beginning of every session, if a musician is not needed until the second half of the program, he or she may decide to show up at intermission. Management has been flexible on this issue, however, there was a concert that included a piano concerto during the first half of the program and a Tchaikovsky symphony, after intermission, on the second half. The associate usually plays the concerto and the principal performs the symphony. As it happened, the soloist was delayed in getting to the hall and the conductor decided to switch the program order. The Tchaikovsky work was now placed on the first half and the concerto on the second half of the program. Since the principal horn player had not yet arrived, the associate principal also had to cover the first horn part in the symphony. Management took advantage of this incident to impress upon musicians the importance of arriving at the hall before the beginning of a concert (whether or not an orchestra member performs during the first or second half of the program).

When a musician is not needed for the entire week of concerts, the player must still remain available just in case of an emergency (illness, accidents, or changes in repertoire).

Morning rehearsals begin sharply at 10:00 a.m. and not at 10:01 or 9:59 a.m. If a conductor decides to begin at 10:01 a.m. (or later), there are no repercussions, but one minute has been lost and cannot be made up. If the session ends at 12:30 p.m., a conductor is not allowed to keep orchestra members onstage until 12:31 p.m. (or later). If this happens, musicians receive a minimum of fifteen minutes overtime pay. To avoid such a situation, the personnel manager enters the stage during the last five minutes of the rehearsal to make sure the conductor finishes on time. If it gets down to thirty seconds and the maestro continues to conduct, the personnel manager approaches the podium and stops the rehearsal. Although the starting time of a concert can be delayed if the audience is not seated, all performances must end within the scheduled time. Contract stipulations differ among orchestras regarding advanced notice to players for overtime and penalties.

Since time is lost when rehearsals do not start promptly and financial consequences incur when they do not end on time, the San Francisco Symphony has placed a clock on both sides of the stage (during rehearsals) to help prevent these occurrences. The maximum length of an average concert (without chorus) is two hours and fifteen minutes. If, for any reason, a program is delayed or a conductor takes a slower tempo, causing the performance to end after the two hour and fifteen minute maximum, the entire onstage orchestra is paid overtime (in fifteen-minute increments).

Tuning is the first order of business at the beginning of every session. All musicians adjust their instruments to the same vibrations per second. For instance, the sound of the note **A** (above Middle **C**) is usually tuned to 440 Hz (cycles per second). Although 440 Hz is taken as the norm, most American orchestras tune a bit higher, up to 444 Hz. The note **A** above Middle **C** was as low as 380 Hz during the middle 18th Century; yet, organs played by Johann Sebastian Bach had the **A** tuned up to 480 Hz. The decision to change an orchestra's pitch has to do with the "brightness" of its sound and can be requested by a music director or a member of the orchestra.

The actual method for tuning varies with orchestras. Formally, the principal oboe sounded the **A** and the entire orchestra tuned up at the same time. The strings complained, however, that the orchestra tuned so loud they could not hear their own instruments. It was then decided that the oboe would play the first **A** for all string players and then another **A** for woodwinds and brass.

The following quote by Bernard Shore, regarding Willem Mengelberg's approach to tuning when he was with the BBC

Symphony Orchestra, comes from David Wooldridge's book, *Conductor's World* (Praeger Publications, Inc., NY):

> *Tuning with him* [Mengelberg] *is a ceremony which may take anything from five minutes to (in extreme cases) two hours. The first violins are directed to take the A only from the first oboe, followed by the seconds (violins), violas, celli and basses. The rest of the orchestra then tunes, starting with the flutes and ending with the tuba. Not until the whole orchestra has the A are the strings allowed to tune their other strings. The oboe officiates like a High Priest, and has to stand and turn to the department concerned, for the benefit of those further away, while Mengelberg, sitting like a Buddha on the rostrum, criticises the slightest deviation in pitch. On the first occasion tuning took twenty-five minutes, and gave rise to his first dissertation:*
> *"It has taken you twenty-five minutes to tune — it should take two minutes! You may be* [a] *first-class orchestra, but if you play not in tune? — It is difficult for musicians — Fifty years ago it did not matter so much perhaps: but now it is necessary to have full house, and if you play not in tune, well — the house will be empty. The first oboe, first clarinet must help their colleagues, like a mother her children: You must watch, like the cat and mouse — there — that little double-bass, you hear him behind there?"*

The situation created by Mengelberg with the BBC Symphony Orchestra would never be tolerated by American orchestras. Although a conductor can address a musician regarding intonation, to treat professional players as though they were in high school would never fly in the United States.

One San Francisco Symphony guest conductor insisted he needed more time to finish a rehearsal. The personnel manager told him the contract (at the time) did not allow overtime without twenty-four hours notice. The conductor, noticeably unhappy, stormed offstage. On a return engagement, several years later, he again requested overtime, which was also denied—he was never invited back.

It is not unusual for a guest conductor or music director to fall out of favor with an orchestra or even patrons; however, it is surprising to see a reaction such as John Beck, Timpanist of the Rochester Philharmonic Orchestra, shares about one of their former music directors:

> *An unpopular Music Director was conducting the Rochester Philharmonic Orchestra and some Eastman School of Music students decided to pull a prank on him during a concert. Somehow they got up into the ceiling above the stage and during the second movement of a Haydn Symphony, they released dozens of ping pong balls upon him and the orchestra. I was playing timpani, but was not playing at that moment, and saw what I thought was dust coming down from the ceiling; however, as they hit the stage, the maestro, and the first violins, I saw them bounce. The Maestro walked off the stage, followed by the concertmaster, and we sat there for what seemed like hours before they returned. The Maestro turned to the audience and said: "Poppa Haydn forgives them!" And we started the symphony over. Irreverent, yes, but it did leave a lasting impression. The Music Director left town shortly after that.*

There is much more involved for orchestra musicians than simply showing up on time. Players require varying amounts of preparation before they can begin a rehearsal or concert. Percussionists, for example, have a large battery of instruments that may be needed for a composition. A contemporary work by John Adams or Charles Wuorinen might require a multiple-percussion onstage setup of ten to twenty instruments—for each percussionist! I usually arrived at Davies Hall one hour early to prepare for a concert. Wind and string players show up fifteen to forty-five minutes early to warm-up (depending on the instrument and player). Preparation is a necessary component of our trade since we must be ready to play, in tune, from the very first note. Some of this time is also used to practice difficult passages that will be rehearsed or performed.

Although symphony musicians practice at home, some need to "feel" the acoustics of their sound within the hall. Oboe, clarinet, and bassoon players have a more complicated situation because of the bamboo reeds that are part of the mouthpiece (clarinetists use one reed; oboists and bassoonists use a double reed). Since the acoustics of a room have much to do with the success (playability) of a reed, woodwind players allocate time before rehearsals and concerts to determine the best one to use. My colleague, Don Carroll, a member of the woodwind section says:

A reed that may be fine for practicing at home, may not work for playing in the Hall. Most clarinetists buy manufactured reeds, and then adjust them by shaving the thin vibrating end with a reed knife. Some professionals make single reeds from blank cane but this is time-consuming and can require special tools. Oboe and bassoon players, advanced and professionals, usually make their own reeds—while beginners and students buy reeds from music supply stores.

Punctuality is an important trait in any business and although an organization will not come to a screeching halt if one employee shows up late, it does show a lack of courtesy towards other workers. For orchestral musicians, especially one-on-a-part players, arriving late for work cannot be tolerated. While on tour in New York, the San Francisco Symphony programmed one of the great Mahler symphonies at Carnegie Hall. Orchestra members were onstage, ready for the 8:00 p.m. concert, when the personnel manager noticed an empty chair. The musician was an extra, substitute player, hired specifically for the tour and, fortunately, his part did not begin until the final movement. The personnel manager called the hotel and when the musician answered the phone, he said he had overslept and rushed to the hall. Since the performance had already begun, he had to walk onstage after the third movement, in front of the entire orchestra, audience, and conductor. He was never hired again!

Although the San Francisco Symphony has a dress code stated in the contract, there are times when jewelry and spangles on clothing can become an issue. When this happens, the personnel manager must judiciously talk to the player to resolve the problem. In times past, there was a Dress Code Committee that formalized rules regarding onstage attire. Men were required to wear black tails (still the case) and women could wear dresses, pantsuits, or a variation of both. The contract, however, contained one stipulation—a dress had to be no more than six inches above the ankle. One woman asked the chair of the players' committee just how high six inches was above the ankle. The point is that it cannot be taken for granted everyone understands or follows directions.

Many years ago, the administration decided to design a dress for women to insure a consistent look—similar to the dress code for men. A dress was made, but after a short trial period women refused to wear it. The main reason was that what looked good on one person did not look good on another. The idea of "messing" with what a woman could or could not wear should have put up a "red flag," and it wasn't long before the entire project was abandoned. As time went on, a few female musicians started to wear men's tailcoats, complete with vest and bowtie. This tradition still continues today. Since there have been so many issues regarding proper stage attire for women, the Symphony contract now spells out what is appropriate:

> *... all black dress or all black blouse and skirt with modest neckline, high back and sleeves to the wrist. Skirt length to be five inches above the ankle or lower, sitting and standing. A white blouse may be worn with a skirt if accompanied by a black jacket with the above neckline, sleeve length, and skirt length. Pant suits, consisting of jacket and tailored pants to the ankle, of matching fabric, may be worn with white or black blouse. Full (men's) dress "tails" may be worn. Hose will be black and shoes should be dressy and all black.*
>
> *The purpose of a dress code is to establish a generally homogenous appearance of the orchestra. To this end the choice of jewelry should be discreet and lace, metallic threads, etc., should be kept at a minimum. (For the purpose of definition, "a minimum" will be defined as trim or ornamentation, e.g., lace sleeves and sequins are not acceptable.) Only small black evening bags may be carried on stage.*

One Symphony President became distracted by several male musicians who wore short socks, exposing part of the leg, during performances. To avoid this attention-grabber, he bought black calf-length socks for all men in the orchestra.

Occasionally, other situations arose that were not covered in the contract; some of them had to do with musicians who ate spicy foods with plenty of garlic. Orchestra members who sat in close proximity to these players complained about the pungent odors but since contract rules did not specifically address what musicians could or could not eat, nothing was able to be done. There were also musicians who used strong perfume or cologne, again causing discomfort to fellow colleagues. Nevertheless, without contract language to address personal issues, the personnel manager has to resolve them in a diplomatic manner. As is evident, it's important to have a sensitive personnel manager who can work with both musicians and management.

Unlike the opera and ballet where the orchestra performs in the pit (recessed stage area) and the "show" takes place onstage—symphony musicians are the show. That's why there is such a long list of rules to insure everyone maintains a consistent look and does not divert the audience's attention from concentrating on the performance.

One of the more unusual examples of a distraction occurred when a cellist (who happened to be a substitute) walked onstage, passing through the bass section, to take her seat for the performance. Bass players lean their instruments upright against stools when they are offstage and as she entered, she accidentally brushed against one of the leaning basses. It fell down, rolled off the stage, and crashed onto the floor in front of the first row of seats. Fortunately, the instrument was able to be repaired but the cellist must still have nightmares about the incident!

A symphony orchestra is an amazing instrument in itself and like a Stradivarius violin, needs gifted players to reach its full potential. When more than one hundred musicians, soloists, and a conductor come together for a performance, they should sound as one voice. This does not happen without the combined efforts of musicians, conductors, composers, the board of directors, administration, staff, stage crew, librarians, fund raisers, and volunteers who coordinate all the behind-the-scenes preparations. Hence, *Rules, Rules, & More Rules* set the guidelines for this profession—for without them, the show could not go on.

RECORDING: "TAKE TWO!"

God tells me how he wants the music played—and you
[the orchestra] *get in the way.*

—Arturo Toscanini

Great musical recordings from the Baroque, Classical, and Romantic Periods, produced by major orchestras around the world, document countless interpretations by a myriad of conductors. Each one defines a particular realization of a composer's score and even though a conductor is charged with the responsibility of creating the basic interpretation, performers add an equal share with their individual sounds and musicianship. Although first-chair players provide the most significant contributions (solo lines), section players also enrich the overall sound of an orchestra.

The production of a compact disc can be compared to writing a book. Authors research, travel, and experience the subject matter before surrendering it to print. The same is true for conductors who spend years proving a score through considerable rehearsals and performances before committing it to a recording. A composer determines the general outline of the music through tempo markings, dynamics, phrasing, articulations, and musical directives (all subject to interpretation) and a conductor provides the overall musical concept of the composer's intentions. Musicians translate, through their instruments, the conductor's directions, gestures, and emotional energy.

A typical recording session takes place in a studio where complete control of acoustics, recording equipment, microphone placement, and playback capabilities are available. Most of today's orchestras choose to record in the familiar surroundings of their own concert halls even though constructing a studio setting out of an auditorium is no small task since it involves the transportation and on-site setup of equipment for all sessions (in addition to a separate room for playbacks). When the San Francisco Symphony recorded for *Decca Records*, the company insisted that a platform be constructed to extend the stage over several front-row seats to create a greater acoustical presence of the orchestra. *Decca Records* wanted more separation between woodwind, brass, percussion, and string sections to allow for a more effective manipulation of the recorded sound. The platform was built (off-site) in ten sections by FM Productions at a cost of $40,000. The extended stage was then shipped and assembled in Davies Hall at an additional cost of $10,000 for each series of recording sessions (not "live" performances).

Michael Tilson Thomas, current Music Director of the San Francisco Symphony, records an entire week of live concerts and then selects the most successful presentation for final release. Before the program begins, he makes an announcement that this evening's performance is being recorded and the audience's part is to be ABSOLUTELY SILENT!

Although performing in front of an audience adds an element of excitement not found in a recording studio, celebrated Chilean pianist, Claudio Arrau, says in *The English Journal, Records and Recording,* that he would not authorize the release of records derived from live concerts since, in his opinion:

> . . . *public auditions provoke stratagems which, having been designed to fill acoustical and psychological requirements of the concert situation, are irritating and anti-architectural when subjected to playbacks.*

His presumption is that well-produced gramophone records are designed for an entirely different kind of listening experience than that encountered in a concert hall.

Before the advent of digital equipment, large sections of music were recorded at a time. If any part was not satisfactory, the entire "take" (section of recorded music) had to be repeated before the conductor and record producer were happy with the results. The digital format now used allows for a few measures of music to be recorded and inserted onto a master disc (even one single note can be replaced on the final edited version). Since live concerts are never perfect, digital editing produces an artificial reproduction of a performance, albeit, a possibly more accurate one. Conductors and musicians realize that performing in front of an audience conveys a level of excitement not found in a studio environment; therefore, many CDs are produced from live performances. The San Francisco Symphony records an entire week of four or five performances, followed by a short "patch" session to adjust for minor details.

In the past, most recordings were made in a studio environment under the American Federation of Musicians Sound Recording Labor Agreement. Rules for studio recording sessions state that only fifteen minutes of music from each hour can be used for the finished product. A forty-five minute composition, therefore, requires a three-hour call. A conductor spends most of the break time listening to playbacks to decide whether or not more takes will be necessary. Musicians, especially principal players with solo parts, listen to their individual contributions, along with the balance of the orchestra as a whole. The conductor and producer, however, get the final say and rarely seek input from orchestra members. Today, recordings are made from live concerts under the Symphony Opera Ballet Live Recording Agreement.

Along with issues of musicianship, tempo, ensemble, and phrasing, there is also the element of extraneous sounds that seem to find their way into a recording. Brass players can inadvertently drop a mute and string players can accidently strike a music stand with a bow—and, anyone can sneeze or cough—all of which can eliminate a take. Percussionists are the most notorious for causing accidental sounds because they are surrounded by so much equipment and are constantly moving around, picking up sticks and mallets from trap tables or the edges of instruments. Cymbals, drums, cowbells, gongs, and other percussion paraphernalia are suspended in front, behind, or on either side of these players—so, it doesn't take much to accidentally drop, strike, kick, or bump into something.

The tambourine, for example, is a very troublesome instrument because it's easy to rattle the jingles. One technique requires the percussionist to turn the tambourine upside down in order to play on the rim instead of on the head. If not done carefully, the jingles can be activated, causing unwanted noise. During a take of *Roman Carnival Overture* by Hector Berlioz, the tambourine player walked offstage to turn it over, hoping to avoid the possibility of making noise. But when he returned to play the part, it was too late—he had missed the entrance! Ironically, that take was chosen for the final mix (master disc). Evidently, no one (except the player) noticed that the tambourine part was missing from those few measures.

The American Federation of Musicians (AFM) sets conditions for sound recordings. A session, for instance, can be scheduled during an orchestra member's day off at the regular rate, however, if it is held between midnight and 8:00 a.m., premium rates go into effect. Recordings scheduled on Sundays are considered different from other free days and musicians will not work on a Sunday unless there is a four-hour minimum call to make it worthwhile. Orchestra members do not receive royalties from the sale of CDs; they are paid an hourly rate set by agreement with the AFM. All American orchestras that record under AFM contracts are paid the same rate. Royalties go directly into the symphony organization's general fund. Some orchestra contracts provide musicians with an additional weekly fee (approximately $30) that entitles management to unlimited live and/or delayed radio broadcasting of recorded performances. If a concert is aired on television, players are paid $80 per hour or $35 per half hour.

Under the direction of Seiji Ozawa, former music director of the San Francisco Symphony, a recording session was scheduled that included the following repertoire: (1) William Russo's *Three Pieces for Blues Band and Symphony Orchestra*, performed with Corky Segel and his Blues Band; (2) *Symphonic Dances from West Side Story* by Leonard Bernstein; (3) *Romeo et Juliette* by Hector Berlioz; (4) *Romeo and Juliet* by Sergei Prokofiev; and (5) *Romeo and Juliet* by Peter Tchaikovsky. Although there were a number of problems during these sessions, I will address one incident that occurred early in the week (with the Russo composition). The Blues Band was placed in front of the stage, surrounded by plastic shields, separating their sound from the orchestra.

The percussion section was situated, as usual, towards the rear of the stage. Ozawa was conducting up front, in close proximity to the band when he addressed the tambourine player, saying the rhythm was not coordinated with the Blues Band. The percussionist, performing the part, had been hired as an extra (substitute) player. I was acting as principal percussionist, playing the mallet parts (xylophone, orchestra bells, and vibraphone). Since the tambourine was becoming such an issue with Ozawa, I decided to switch with the substitute player for this section of the music. But Ozawa was still unhappy—now with me—saying the rhythm was still late (behind the band). Yet, to my ears, it sounded just fine. In my opinion, the most likely solution was to have the tambourine player (whose rhythm accompanied the Blues Band) move to the front of the stage where the band was located because playing in the back of the orchestra caused the tambourine to sound delayed on the recording. But, this was not done and the session went into overtime, and Ozawa was upset.

Ozawa's response to this and other issues during the recording was to discharge seven musicians, not just for the Russo piece, but the entire session. I received a call from the personnel manager at midnight, telling me I would be replaced, along with the extra percussionist, principal viola, harp, pianist, principal cello, and principal trumpet. Although all of these long-standing and highly-trained professional musicians had been contracted to play the recording, Ozawa was within his legal rights to dismiss us (without loss of pay) and hire substitutes. Union regulations permit any member of the Federation to be hired for a recording under the International Agreement. But, such a recording atmosphere is not conducive to producing an inspired performance.

Orchestra members demand tenure as part of their contract because, without it, unfair dismissal of competent musicians can take place at the whim of music directors. When new directors are hired, they want to put their own stamp on an orchestra by bringing in players of their choosing, nevertheless, most wait until openings occur through the normal channels of retirement, injury, or death and then hold auditions to fill these open positions. In the meantime, they usually work with musicians to obtain the results they desire. But if a musician falls out of favor with a music director, the usual procedure is to call a meeting to discuss the particular problem and to try and improve the situation. If no solution can be found, the director is at liberty to reseat the player to a different chair. The player, however, can appeal the decision through provisions in the contract.

When Saul Goodman was timpanist of the New York Philharmonic, he made it a point to tell his students how demanding it was to work for Arturo Toscanini, the Orchestra's Music Director. He said Toscanini screamed at players, sang out in a high-pitched voice, danced on the podium, and used any method possible to capture the music's intent. But, Goodman also said Toscanini never fired anyone—even though tenure was unheard of in those days.

Recordings are, by far, the most stressful of performing situations for musicians because every note is scrutinized, not only by the conductor, but by recording company personnel who intently follow the score as though they are listening through a stethoscope. During the usual four rehearsals before a subscription (regular series) concert, musicians prepare themselves to rehearse passages of music with different articulations, dynamics, and phrasing. A conductor will go over certain passages, again and again, until he or she is completely satisfied with the musical results. During a live performance, however, if things do not go as planned, there is no going back to make corrections. Every take in a recording session is similar to a live performance and if a mistake or mishap occurs in intonation or rhythm, musicians have to repeat those sections over and over again. In other words, professional players are expected to perform every take with absolute perfection. This is especially challenging for the brass section when they must play at extremely high ranges.

During a regular concert series of dramatic works such as the Mahler symphonies (which can last for more than an hour), musicians are able to pace themselves, knowing where climaxes occur and when to rest between entrances. In other words, they are mentally and physically prepared for the demands of the score. Studio recording (not live performances) adds a greater amount of stress because players never know when any given passage will be satisfactory—for example, the brass section may have played well but the woodwinds might have had problems. Trying to create a perfect take, consequently, can result in tiring an orchestra and cause musicians to lose their edge. The pressure of repeating passages of music with the same enthusiasm, passion, artistry, and technically-perfect execution, again and again, is very challenging.

On the flip side, when a solo player or an entire section has trouble, a second chance can be a most-welcomed opportunity to "get it right."

This backstage glimpse of what takes place during the recording process of a major symphony orchestra should give the reader a greater appreciation for the final product—those magnificent CDs that provide music aficionados with so much pleasure. If musicians had it their way, I believe they would prefer to record in the comfort and acoustically-familiar surroundings of their normal working environment, onstage, during an actual concert situation, instead of in a studio setting where *Take Two* can easily turn into *Takes Three, Four,* or more!

TOURING: NEXT STOP ... VIENNA

Music is the universal language of mankind.

—Henry Wadsworth Longfellow

A ny discussion of a great symphony orchestra has to include touring. In part, touring is a status symbol that acknowledges an orchestra's greatness because it dares to perform 18th and 19th Century symphonic literature throughout the world for audiences and critics who have heard this same repertoire played by other distinguished orchestras. This is especially true in Europe where many famous composers were born. Touring orchestras maintain an international presence that elevates them to "world-class" standing. Yet, what is the definitive proof that an orchestra has risen to such a level? The answer lies in reviews published by foreign newspapers. The public relations department of an American orchestra devours these seemingly irrefutable expressions of unsurpassed magnitude, penned by music critics, and reprinted in local newspapers, highlighting its magniloquence for adoring patrons—who believe every word!

Touring does not generate net earnings for an orchestra and, conversely, these out-of-country adventures are exceedingly expensive to produce. Although an orchestra may find sponsors for international tours, for the most part, all costs are born primarily by ticket sales and the orchestra's general fund. Conductors encourage touring and are most willing to share their musical interpretations on the international stage because it raises their own personal world-class status which, they hope, will further enhance their careers. Most musicians also subscribe to a touring philosophy and are eager to perform for sophisticated audiences in major music halls around the world.

Nothing brings members of an orchestra closer together than spending several weeks on the road. Sharing meals, sightseeing, and hours on buses, trains, and planes all create long-lasting, bonding relationships in this great family.

Touring with a music director, his or her entourage, one hundred musicians, a stage manager and crew, a librarian, administrative personnel, a physician, and two travel agents for a period of three or four weeks (minimum time required to justify expenses for a foreign tour) is a monumental feat. At the forefront of these expenses is transportation. Major American orchestra contracts stipulate that management must provide first-class travel arrangements for orchestra personnel and although it's not possible to have this classification for all one hundred people on airplanes, management is required to secure, when available, first-class accommodations on trains, buses, and hotels. Chartered flights are sometimes necessary to meet scheduling demands.

Transporting instruments on tour is of top priority and adds considerably to travel expenses. Customized trunks must be fabricated to protect this valuable cargo while in transit. Some players will not even allow their personal instruments to be packed in trunks because of its intrinsic value (amounting to hundreds of thousands of dollars), many of which are irreplaceable. For this reason, musicians will not let their instruments out of sight and treat them as carry-on baggage whenever possible. During custom inspections at border crossings, however, this cargo has to be declared by symphony management. Orchestra members and management have agreed to ship this expensive freight in a climate-controlled environment to avoid any damage from extreme weather conditions. Temperature gauges, therefore, are packed into trunks so musicians can be assured instruments have not been subjected to extreme heat or cold.

Once an orchestra arrives at its destination, a local trucking company takes responsibility for transporting all symphony cargo to tour venues. With as many as five days of consecutive travel to different cities, and depending on distance and mode of transportation, instruments may have to be transferred overnight by truck while orchestra personnel travel by plane during the day.

Hotel reservations are another complex issue for touring orchestras. As stated before, the symphony contract stipulates that musicians are to be provided with first-class hotel accommodations, and although individual rooms are provided for all members, some players choose to share rooms with other performers. In this case, management does not have to book two rooms and passes the savings on to musicians. Each player, therefore, receives one-third the price of the room not used. Musicians who book lodging at other hotels or stay with friends or relatives are compensated for the entire cost of the hotel room. One important consideration when choosing a roommate is to be sure the person does not snore since there is nothing worse than losing a night's sleep when on the road!

Some orchestra members have special requests, such as, bed type, smoking or non-smoking rooms, accommodations on a high floor (to avoid noise) or below the seventh floor (for fire and other safety reasons), and pillows without down feathers. Orchestra members are also allowed to bring family members or guests on a tour (at their own expense). But, when one considers management has already paid for the player's hotel room and the daily per diem allowance can be stretched to include most meals, transportation is literally the only additional cost.

Management also accommodates orchestra personnel by collecting luggage outside the hotel room (by midnight) before departure the following day and places it in the next hotel room upon arrival in the new city. Although this is very convenient for orchestra personnel, it does add to tour expenses. All of these details make for very complicated travel arrangements.

My wife and our two children travelled with the San Francisco Symphony to Europe and Russia for six weeks and to Japan for three weeks. In fact, our children were the very first ones to travel as dependents. Touring with an orchestra family, sleeping in a different hotel almost every night, eating ethnic foods, and learning foreign-language words was an exciting experience for our youngsters. We still laugh about the time my wife ordered oatmeal for Anthony and Liz in a Belgian cafe. The waiter brought us eggs but all the children received were two glasses of warm milk. After a while, my wife asked the server where the oatmeal was and he pointed to the milk, saying: "Yes, goat milk." It must have been her New York accent!

A physician always accompanies an orchestra on foreign tours and medical services are available to symphony personnel, guests, and dependents at no charge. Management does, however, ask that pertinent medical information be provided.

An orchestra member's entire salary is paid in advance of a tour (a convenience to those who remain at home). The daily per-diem allowance includes money for breakfast ($20), lunch ($30), dinner ($35), and miscellaneous items ($20). Since most meals are eaten in costly hotel restaurants (because of time constraints), the per diem is quite substantial at $105 per day. And, although a player can decide to eat a Big Mac and fries and pocket the saved money, most musicians are eager to try the wide variety of exotic foods offered in foreign countries. When the San Francisco Symphony performs in New York City, orchestra members receive an additional $20 per day because of this City's high cost of living. Foreign tour per diem is calculated differently. Orchestra members are paid the same rate established by the General Services Administration, a Federal Agency that sets per-diem rates for government travel. Justification for such expensive tours is directly related to the publicity it generates. Tour reviews provide symphony patrons an opportunity to follow an orchestra's international exploits (which increase future ticket sales at home). When an orchestra performs in a fascinating country or famous concert hall, the publicity helps solicit donations for its yearly fund-raising activities and also increases CD sales; however, symphony organizations rarely recoup touring costs (or recording expenses, for that matter).

A typical three-week foreign tour costs approximately $3 million, not including the musicians' weekly salaries. Concert fees (or ticket sales) can bring in up to $2,500,000, leaving a deficit of approximately $500 thousand which must be made up from the general fund or raised by corporate and/or individual sponsors. It is also important to understand that weeks spent on the road reduce revenue from concerts that would have been performed at home.

At first, visiting a foreign country is very exciting but after years of touring, the glamour can wear off and all that is left is a grueling work schedule. A usual tour day begins early in the morning with management, musicians, dependants, and guests, boarding a bus to the airport or train station (the conductor usually travels separately). After a short flight (or long bus or train ride), there is only a few hours of free time to sightsee or take a nap before locating a decent restaurant for dinner and to prepare for the evening performance. After the concert, some musicians "hang out" to wind down while others head straight back to the hotel to rest up for the same, next-day itinerary. This hectic schedule can go on for four or five consecutive days before the orchestra receives a welcomed day off.

Some musicians practice an hour or more before a concert. This can present a problem, depending on a player's roommate or the person who occupies the adjacent room. One year, I happened to be next to the principal bassoon player. The evening's program included *The Rite of Spring* by Igor Stravinsky. The bassoonist practiced the extremely difficult opening measures for at least an hour—over, and over, and over again. Although there is no way to know who will be next door, choosing a roommate can become very serious business for touring musicians. That's why many principal players prefer private lodging.

André Previn, pianist and conductor, sums up the subject of touring quite well in his book, *Orchestra* (Doubleday and Company, Inc., New York):

> *Now let me examine the problems of touring with an orchestra for a bit. To the layman, the presence of an orchestra on a stage is a matter which is taken for granted. The mountainous problems of actually getting that orchestra to the stage must be kept from an audience. Think about it: one hundred or more players to transport around the world, together with all*

the instruments, the music library, the administrative staff, accompanying members of the Press, wives and friends. Planes to charter, train tickets to book, coaches to hire, adequate hotel accommodations to see to, travel time not to exceed a certain amount of hours a day, restaurants to find while on the road, local managements to sort out, foreign currency to reckon with, per diem payments to the players, acoustical problems in the various concert halls, adequate seating arrangements in these auditoriums, local receptions to cope with—the list goes on and on. It is a miracle that tours happen at all.

The financial problems are truly staggering, and with the rising costs of everything it has become an almost insolvable muddle. I have toured with quite a few orchestras during my career: the Louisiana Symphony Orchestra, the Pittsburgh Symphony, the Vienna, the Chicago, and the Royal Philharmonic. There is nothing in life quite comparable to life on tour. On the average, six concerts a week are played, and with few exceptions, each one in a different city.

On May 15, 1973, the San Francisco Symphony embarked upon its first European tour with an initial program in Paris at the Théâtre des Champs Elysées (famous for the world premiere of Igor Stravinsky's *The Rite of Spring*). Our concert was the first to be broadcast live via satellite on KKHI-FM in San Francisco. And, although there have been many magical moments during my career, this performance surpassed them all. As a young musician, in the great City of Paris, in such a magnificent concert hall, and with Seiji Ozawa, conducting *Symphonie Fantastique* by Hector Berlioz, it was a concert I will never forget.

After leaving Paris, the orchestra continued on to Belgium, England, Switzerland, Germany, Austria, and Italy, with its final concerts in Leningrad (St. Petersburg), Vilnius (Lithuania), and Moscow.

Leningrad (as it was known then) was a drab and uninspiring City (as was much of Russia at that time). Yet, visiting the grand museums, cathedrals, and palaces from the reign of Peter the Great (18th Century), when Leningrad was known as St. Petersburg, was a great adventure. One of the tour highlights was The Hermitage, the largest art museum in the world, housing European paintings and sculptures in 120 rooms from the 13th to 20th Centuries.

Another Russian treasure was the Summer Palace of Peter the Great and although it was not very large (fourteen rooms), it was still magnificent with its 1500 acres of formal gardens and 173 fountains. Peter's sense of humor was evident with his many fountains disguised as metal trees. When guests stepped on triggers hidden in the ground, the fountains were activated and doused visitors with water.

One dreary, rainy morning, my family and I left the Leningrad Hotel to board a bus, along with the entire orchestra, as we headed to the airport. Upon arrival, all Symphony personnel were escorted to a ground-level waiting room for the trip to Lithuania. Since the airport had no jet ways (passenger boarding bridges) to connect terminals with planes, we had to walk on the tarmac (in a heavy rain storm) to the aircraft which was about one hundred yards away. When the front of the line reached the plane, we saw them stop, turn, and change direction, now heading towards a different aircraft, much further away. Obviously, we had been led to the wrong plane! When they reached the second aircraft, everyone huddled under the wings to keep dry since the rolling set of stairs had not arrived. When it finally did come, an airport security guard climbed up to open the door but, believe it or not, it was locked and she did not have a key! By this time everyone was noticeably frustrated.

Once inside the cabin, it was obvious Russian aircraft was nothing like what we were accustomed to in America or Europe. The airplane, provided by Aeroflot (the only Russian carrier), looked like a World War II reject with portholes for windows. There were no tray tables for reading, eating, or other amenities and, to make matters worse, a truck pulled up alongside the plane and a woman, wearing a babushka, jumped out, hopped onto the wing, and filled it with fuel. We soon realized we were no longer under FAA regulations. No door separated passengers from the cockpit so everyone had a full view of the pilot and co-pilot. The only partition was, what seemed to be, a shower curtain with a few missing rings. As the plane took off, a loose wire began to fly around in the cockpit, sparking as it hit the walls. The flight attendant, aware of what was happening, quickly closed the curtain, and off we went up into the "WILD Blue Yonder," men and women white-knuckling the arm rests! Our children, too young to be aware of what was taking place, enjoyed the two hour, roller-coaster ride. Adults were quite concerned that the plane would go up in flames and it was only by the grace of God that we finally landed at our destination in Lithuania.

On the final leg of the tour, management asked if anyone was willing to take an overnight train ride to Moscow since there were not enough available seats on the plane for the entire orchestra. My wife and I were the first to raise our hands and we had a very enjoyable trip.

The highlight of the Moscow concerts was a performance in the Great Hall of the Moscow Conservatory with Mstislav Rostropovich who performed the Dvořák *Cello Concerto*. The fact that Rostropovich had been banned from concertizing in his homeland (because of his friendship with Aleksandr Solzhenitsyn and other dissidents) added to the elevated excitement of the evening.

Moscow is noted for Red Square with its towers of Spasskaya (the main gate to the Kremlin), Senatskaya (a defensive military structure), Nikolskaya (named after the Nikolsky Greek Monastery), St. Basil's Cathedral, and the Cathedral of Vasily the Blessed, all of which overlook the monuments to Kuzma Minin and Dmitry Pozharsky (national heroes), the State Historical Museum, the famous Gum Department Store, and Lenin's Mausoleum where, since his death in 1924, his body has been on display. As we entered the tomb, my son asked me a question. A guard, holding a machine gun, looked him straight in the eye and said in a gruff voice, "No talking!" After that, the line couldn't move fast enough for us.

While visiting one of the magnificent palaces in Russia, I inadvertently dropped my passport. On the way out, a colleague informed me that it was being held at the office. I was fortunate to have retrieved it because a violinist also lost his passport and the Russian government delayed his departure for three days before the American Embassy settled the matter.

As stated before, touring American orchestras are contracted to have first-class hotel accommodations; however, when booking this tour, management did not realize Russia's system with regard to room and board since their category of services ranged from Super Deluxe to Deluxe to First Class. In other words, the San Francisco Symphony, by booking first class, actually contracted for third-class accommodations. This meant all meals were catered in a large dining room instead of in an intimate restaurant setting. Dinners consisted of fried meat, potatoes, and cucumbers (most meals) with carbonated water as the only beverage since no other drinks were allowed to be purchased. Dependents and guests, on the other hand, were booked at the super-deluxe rate by Intourist, the Russian Travel Agency, which, according to U.S. standards, was truly first class. Travelling companions dined separately from musicians, enjoying caviar, fresh vegetables, local Russian cuisine, a variety of beverages, and desserts. When I finished my meal, I would hurry to the restaurant where my wife and children were eating, looking for leftovers! Once management realized what had happened, they tried to upgrade the orchestra's food service but

Russian government officials would not entertain any change in the contractual agreement.

Morris Lang, a member of the New York Philharmonic, shares his "tongue-in-cheek" review of food served at the famous *Rossiya Hotel* in Moscow during a tour with his orchestra under this "third-class" accommodation. This is the same large dining room I described above:

> For openings, try the succulent fish plate. The delicately sliced smoked fish was a bit dry on one tasting, but continued to improve for the next eleven days. The garnish of ripe Romanian tomatoes and skillfully peeled cucumbers added a touch of freshness. The delicate horseradish sauce was only served on Tuesday, Thursday, and Saturday. The lukewarm chicken soup smelled like the real thing, is nicely seasoned with salt, but alas, there is little evidence that a chicken dropped in for a visit. The main courses tried were distinctly native. The crispy Chicken Kiev was deep fat fried and oozing with melted butter. It is strongly recommended by the accounting department of the American Medical Association. Beef Stroganoff is named after Count Stroganoff who, after a successful assassination attempt, fell face down into a pitcher of heavy cream. The boiled fish was an attempt by Peter the Great to bring healthy food to Russia. Fech! – we don't eat healthy food.
>
> The restaurant is distinguished by the great variety of vegetables available. As the band gently played the "Vulgar Boatman" and "Georgia on My Mind," I sampled the Sweet and Sour Potatoes, Potatoes al Dente, Sugared Potatoes, Mashed Potatoes, Honey Coated Potatoes, and Russian Fries. All are recommended!

The beverage list is somewhat limited, although the few selections are excellent. Try the "74" Fanta, and for a new taste thrill, roll the imported Leningrad mineral water around the tongue.

It's not unusual for local symphony musicians to visit backstage with their American counterparts. During this tour, a member of the Moscow Philharmonic Percussion Section visited the San Francisco Symphony percussionists. Since he did not speak English, an interpreter translated the conversation. As a sign of friendship, I gave him some of my published percussion compositions. He was very appreciative and told me he would come back tomorrow to present me with a gift of a Russian Samovar (an elaborate device that boils water for tea). When he didn't show up, I wondered what had happened. Eventually, I learned that it was illegal for Russian citizens to give Samovars to foreigners. For all I know, the translator (rumored to be a Russian spy) may have turned him in to the "Authorities" and shipped him off to Siberia!

Years later, a Russian percussion student enrolled in my studio at San Jose State University. During his course of study, I suggested he perform my *Sonata for Timpani and Piano* as one of his recital pieces. He proceeded to tell me how famous this sonata was in his country, saying many percussionists had a copy of it. I told him the story of how I gave it to a member of the Moscow

Philharmonic. He said it was probably copied and circulated throughout the years. So much for royalties!

After a concert in a foreign country, members of local orchestras occasionally invite American musicians out for a drink. My colleague, Laurie McGaw, shares a story about his experience with some brass players while in Russia:

> *When we performed in Leningrad, the Leningrad Philharmonic was on tour; however, members of the other orchestra in town, the Leningrad Symphony, called on us at the concert hall. We brass players were invited to come to a party following our concert. Several of us went. The party consisted of many toasts back and forth, with each participant expected to down his drink completely without stopping for air. Some of our members tried to keep up with the Russians, but couldn't without paying a heavy price. One of our players was so inebriated, he actually slid (literally!) under the table.*

The performances in Russia were very well received. There weren't many American orchestras touring the USSR during the Cold War Period and the music-loving public treated us with great enthusiasm and sold-out concerts. Music transcends all worldly discord and whether it is religion, politics, culture, or oral communication, this universal language speaks to everyone—not simply with words—but emotions.

On a yearly tour to Carnegie Hall in New York City, two colleagues and I were walking down Seventh Avenue in Midtown Manhattan. I'm sure we looked like out-of-town tourists, checking out the sights along the way. As we walked south, two men headed north towards us. When they got closer, they split up, each one moving towards the outside of the three of us. One man was carrying a white plastic take-out box of food. He bumped into my friend, causing the food to fall on the sidewalk. The guy went "ape" and blamed my friend for ruining his meatball sandwich. The scam artist insisted that my colleague pay for his lunch and went into a tirade, screaming and waving his hands in the air. Thinking he was going to start a fight, my friend took out his wallet and gave him $5 to avoid getting punched. The man then knelt down, scooped up the sandwich from the sidewalk, and set out to look for more suckers. This has forever become known as the "New York Meatball Scam."

During the late 1980s, when terrorism began to show up at American Embassies and other random spots around the world, Symphony management asked the Federal Government to present a workshop for orchestra members so they could be better prepared during suspicious situations in foreign countries. Among other things, they taught us how to lift our hands in a defensive manner and to turn and run if approached by strangers. This advice came in handy during a visit to Frankfurt, Germany. My colleague, Don Carroll (bass clarinet) and I were not needed for the evening concert (thank God for Beethoven and Brahms who didn't write very often for percussion and bass clarinet), so we decided to tour the City for the entire day. We were warned not to walk near the Main River after dark, but since we had spent so much time on the other side, when we were ready to head back to the hotel, it was already dark and the street bordering the river was now lined with parked cars. As we proceeded, I noticed a car door slowly opening about fifty feet in front of us (which looked suspicious). I mentioned it to my colleague and said: "Let's cross the street and run!" That's exactly what we did. When I looked back, I saw a man had emerged from the back seat and was looking in the direction we had been walking. By the time he realized what had happened, we were far away. I'm sure we avoided being mugged or harmed in some way. Yet, considering all the touring we have done, there have been very few negative incidents.

The saying, *It's a Small World,* is never more evident than when on tour. I've run into students and friends in many countries. In fact, while in Dresden, East Germany, as I walked past the hotel pool, my next-door neighbor called out to me—neither one of us knew we were travelling in Europe and couldn't believe the coincidence of meeting in this way.

Touring, while very demanding, does provide musicians with a cosmopolitan perspective of the profession. Every country is unique and audiences are usually very accepting of an American orchestra's visit. Our perception as performers is also enriched by the powerful influence music has on all world cultures.

When on such a tedious, continuous schedule, days blur into one another, making it easy for musicians and orchestra personnel to lose track of time and place. This may be one reason why management provides all touring personnel with pocket-size books that detail the day's activities. All we have to do is turn a page to know where we are, what time to board a bus, train, or plane, and when the concert begins. So, the first thing I do every morning is open this little black book to be sure the next stop on the itinerary is truly Vienna!

CRUEL AND UNMUSICAL

*The public doesn't want new music; the main thing it
demands of a composer is that he be dead.*

—Arthur Honegger

Contemporary music has always had a place in symphonic
repertoire and although the majority of music performed
today comes from the Classical and Romantic Periods (18th and
19th Centuries), conductors and management are also committed
to program works from the 20th and 21st Centuries. Patrons, for the
most part, do not share this sentiment, wanting to hear the "war
horses" of the 19th Century (Beethoven, Brahms, Tchaikovsky,
and so forth). Consequently, as Honegger alludes in the above
quote, there is not much interest in the works of living composers.
Within the category of contemporary music, this chapter considers
the *avant-garde*. Orchestra members are split on this subject, with
some who enjoy the challenge of performing new music and others who have no interest in playing or listening to *avant-garde* compositions—considering it a heartache! A San Francisco Symphony
musician who sat in the first violin section actually "booed" a
performance during the applause of a particularly irritating *avant-
garde* work—to the dismay of management. Although musicians

may not be fond of a particular composition or a conductor's interpretation of a score, it is the player's responsibility to perform what has been programmed. As musicians, our opinions regarding repertoire are not sought out by management, conductors, or patrons; rather, these judgments are left to professional music critics.

During the early 1900s, composers began to experiment with harmonic and rhythmic elements of classical music, challenging the extreme ranges and dynamics of instruments. They moved away from 2/4, 3/4, 4/4, and 6/8 time signatures into mixed meters, expanding the tonic-dominant relationship of chord progressions while, at the same time, retaining the traditional elements of structure and form. By the 1940s, however, there was also a transformation away from melody and traditional harmonies into more abstract musical dissonance. Composers became more adventurous and by the 1970s, rhythm, melody, and tone centers (major and minor keys) were avoided altogether, replaced by a more mechanical approach to composing that included sound clusters (groups of notes in intervals of seconds) with no pure rhythmic pulse.

Performers were no longer required to create beautiful melodies, using the resonant vibrations cultivated through years of practice; instead, composers found ways to extract the most bizarre and obscure effects. Musicians were even asked to perform in nontraditional ways, for example, string players had to repeat a single note with harsh bowing techniques (usually reserved for the percussion section) and to use their fist or bow to knock or strike the body of the instrument. Wind players were instructed to hum or screech through mouthpieces in order to produce ungodly sounds.

Percussionists were given "new" instruments to strike: automobile brake drums, tin cans, metal blocks, bottles, garbage can lids, and water glasses (to name a few). They were also asked to generate eerie, high-pitched, screeching sounds from cymbals and tam tams by rubbing the surfaces with metal or plastic beaters or to submerge a gong in a tub of water (after being struck) to "bend" the sound. During one composition, I was asked to dump a pail of broken glass into another empty pail, at a precise moment in the composition, to create a particularly opprobrious effect.

No longer was it necessary for musicians to play rhythms with the precision of a metronome. These *avant-garde* composers simply wrote a series of notes (with no rhythmic value) to be performed within a given time frame and players were asked to improvise without regard to pitch or rhythm (not to mention intonation). In other words, instruments were used to create effects without considering the musical artistry it took players a lifetime to perfect.

Yet, these composers were actually quite inventive as they tried to move away from the traditional concepts of orchestral compositions. The problem, however, as I see it, was more related to a loss of passion and expression in the music. Complex rhythms and sound clusters may have tickled the ears of some players but did nothing for the soul, leaving performers with an intellectual challenge while denying them an emotional outlet. I believe it was especially difficult for audiences because they were not able to experience the physical demands that were required to perform these compositions, and without an internal and emotional connection to the music, patrons were left in a void of chaotic, unsystematic and, at times, inexorable displays of disjunctive clatter. The era of the *avant-garde* experience came on too fast and without the necessary preparation for the general public.

Leonard Bernstein, former Music Director of the New York Philharmonic, commented in the Introduction to his book, *The Infinite Variety of Music,* that for the first time in history musical life was no longer based on compositions of the time but on music from past centuries (Simon and Schuster, NY):

> *We could conceivably look at this drastic change with equanimity, form a quasi-scientific opinion about its causes, and even project an objective theory as to its probable future course—if it were not for the fact that we are simultaneously living with such an incredible boom in musical activity. Statistics are soaring: more people are listening to more music than ever before. And it is the intersection of these two phenomena—the public's enormous new interest in music, plus their total lack of interest in **new** music, the musical bang plus the musical whimper—that has created this scary moment.*
>
> *I am a fanatic music lover. I can't live one day without hearing music, playing it, studying it, or thinking about it. And in this role of simple music lover, I confess, freely though unhappily, that at this moment, as of this writing, God forgive me, I have far more pleasure in following the musical adventures of Simon & Garfunkel or of The Association singing "Along Comes Mary" than I have in most of what is being written now by the whole community of "avant-garde" composers.*

Another commentary regarding the *avant-garde* influence on contemporary music comes from the famous Danish composer, conductor, and violinist, Carl Nielsen, in *Living Music* (Wilhelm Hansen Musik, Copenhagen):

> *Here we are at the heart—or rather, the rotten core—of the contemporary conception of art. We are experiencing a strange, impotent, abnormal tendency to mix the arts one with another: a singularly perverse craving to see what will come out of the most absurd conglomeration. It is not a sane breeder's attempt to improve his strains, but a queer, emasculate desire to see monsters.*

French writer and poet, André Breton, best known as the principal founder of surrealism, has a suggestion for *avant-garde* composers in an article entitled, *Music is Dangerous/Silence is Golden* (First published in *Modern Music Magazine*, March-April, 1944. Translated by Louise Varèse):

> *It is evident then that poets, in spite of their lack of comprehension, have gone a long way on the only road, which in such times as these, is great and sure: that of a return to principles. This I should like to point out to musicians. However, for want of a common vocabulary, perhaps I will be unable to measure **their** steps toward those who with them, in order to revive it must share some of the virgin soil of sound.*

In a July, 1933 letter, Arturo Toscanini makes a comment about contemporary music after, once again, reviewing the score to Bach's *B Minor Mass* in Harvey Sachs' *The Letters of Arturo Toscanini* (Random House, Inc., NY):

> *Most modern composers, even if they are good musicians, have no internal voice to listen to; no revelation comes to them from a world of the spirit, as it came to Bach, Beethoven, and Wagner! Poor wretches, why do they continue to daub at paper?*

Lou Harrison shares his philosophy of music in the simplicity of just one verse in his *Joys and Perplexities — Selected Poems of Lou Harrison* (The Jargon Society, Winston-Salem, NC):

> *Melody is the grace of music and the beauty of its work.*

Lou Harrison and I were colleagues for 17 years at San José State University. During that time, I conducted many of his compositions with my percussion ensemble. In 1973, I asked five faculty members to write a new work for a concert of world premieres I was planning. At that time, Lou composed his famous *Concerto for Organ with Percussion Orchestra*. As a tribute to our years of collaboration, he later wrote a solo for tenor bells (a prominent instrument in his American Gamelan), entitled *Solo for Anthony Cirone*. The following quote is taken from an article about this piece by Brady Spitz (*Appreciating Lou Harrison: Performance as Creation in "Solo for Anthony Cirone,"* Percussive Notes, Vol. 49, No. 2):

Harrison found himself looking backwards for much of his career. He was infatuated with the music from 1250-1750 and fluent in much of the music of the world. Following his whims and own aesthetic sense of purity backward, he was led beyond modernism. And, as Peter Garland puts it, "Stepping out of, and beyond modernism has been one of the most impor-tant and radical acts any composer in this century has taken." (The Music of Lou Harrison — Some Biographical Perspectives [A Preface] from *A Lou Harrison Reader,* ed. Peter Garland, Santa Fe, NM: Soundings Press.)

All of these writers show great emotion, wisdom, and insight into the state of *avant-garde* music and although there is much to be said for its innovation, vision, originality, and creativity, composers might also consider the reactions musicians and patrons have with regard to their works when a listener's sensibilities are being attacked by music devoid of qualities that make it great— melody, rhythm, and harmony.

Once the San Francisco Symphony made a commitment to program *avant-garde* music on the regular subscription series, they had to "sell" it to the public. When it was introduced, audiences booed and wrote letters, threatening to cancel subscriptions if it continued. Management, therefore, was forced to schedule a sepa-rate series of performances to feature this new wave of contempo-rary music. Since these programs could not be held in the regular concert hall (which accommodated almost three thousand people), a smaller venue was found to seat a few hundred patrons. The hope was to find an audience larger than the number of players onstage! The first series of *avant-garde* music, *Musica Viva,* began in the mid 1960s and was directed by Aaron Copland. During the ensuing years, the name changed to *New & Unusual Music,* but musicians quickly re-titled it to *Cruel & Unmusical!* Years later, a third series was formed, *Wet Ink,* so named because the music hardly had a chance to dry on manuscript paper before it was performed.

A composition by George Crumb called *Echoes of Time and the River* was programmed on one of the regular subscription series and although it included a number of unusual effects, was actually very well written. The score called for small groups of players to be clustered onstage with some of them moving around during the performance. At one point, three clarinetists marched (while playing) from one side of the stage to the other. The clarinetist who led the group was a bit uncoordinated and found it difficult to march and play at the same time. So, instead of moving in step with the other performers, he swayed, similar to a giraffe's gait, which was quite humorous to watch.

Crumb's score also required a large tub of water and a small gong. A percussionist, after striking the gong, had to submerge it into a tub of water to bend the tone (producing an unusual effect). Although it was the stage crew's responsibility to set up the tub of water for every rehearsal and concert, they thought it was ridiculous and were not happy with the assignment. During the first performance, just as the percussionist was about to submerge the gong in water, he noticed a goldfish swimming around. (Orchestra members could tell something was going on by the expression on his face.) As he struck the gong and lowered it into the tub, the vibrations that emanated from the instrument caused the fish to panic and frantically swim in all directions. The percussionist had a hard time keeping his composure and by the end of the work, the goldfish was dead! The stage crew (responsible for the prank) thought it was hilarious. Fortunately, the conductor and audience had no idea what had taken place.

Without question, the most unusual event of my career happened at a small theater in San Francisco during one of the *New & Unusual* concerts. I will relate the story without mentioning any names to protect the guilty! One of the compositions on the program was by a German composer, Hauber-Stock Ramadi. The work called for a male vocalist and chamber orchestra. The soloist read lines from the play, *Waiting for Godot*, by Samuel Beckett, making weird sounds as he spoke. Minutes before the piece began, a percussion section colleague told me the pianist was going to play a musical ditty (*da da dee dum dee dum*), at the conclusion of the composition and that all percussionists should add a "clunk" after the final note. I thought he was kidding, but at the conclusion of the "experience" (I refuse to call it music), while the audience applauded, the following sequence of events took place:

1. The pianist played the ditty with only two of the three percussionists adding the final "clunk" (one on a chime and the other on a cymbal). There were only two players because I froze, standing there with a snare drum stick and a cowbell in my hands. For those who are able to read music, this is how it sounded:

2. When the soloist heard it, he stormed offstage, throwing his music at the pianist on the way out.
3. The pianist, shocked by the soloist's display of anger, also ran offstage.
4. The entire orchestra began to laugh.
5. The audience, not understanding what had happened, continued to applaud, thinking it was part of the "experience."
6. At the end of the program, the orchestra manager (who was at the concert), not believing what had transpired, reprimanded the only full-time, tenured orchestra member of the three musicians.
7. The pianist and one of the percussionists who participated in the *ad-lib* Coda were extra (substitute) players. They were never hired again. (Actually this is not entirely true because the pianist was hired, many years later, as a guest conductor.)
8. The other player, a member of the orchestra, was fined.

All I can say in defense of these players is that when classical musicians are asked to perform such egregious works, temporary insanity sets in.

I was sitting backstage one day during a rehearsal of a new *avant-garde* composition with highly-complex rhythms and very little melody when the elevator door opened and a Symphony staff member came out. Hearing strange sounds emanating from the hall, she asked me why the orchestra was tuning up. To her astonishment, I told her it was a rehearsal of a new *avant-garde* work. With such complex music, there is not much difference between random and organized chaos. When an orchestra tunes up after taking the **A** from the oboe, they play scales, test high and low notes, practice an excerpt or a virtuoso passage from a concerto, and hearing all of this in unison results in pandemonium. In some instances, *avant-garde* composers actually try to create organized confusion—many of whom succeed! A music critic once tried to convince management to have the orchestra remain silent after tuning to the **A** because of the resulting turmoil. Ironically, he was a champion of the *avant-garde*.

Eventually, the turmoil of the 1970s subsided and contemporary composers moved away from non-melodic and non-rhythmic attempts of composing music. Instead, they began to incorporate interesting new harmonies with complex rhythmic structures into their compositions. By returning elements of melodic passion, artistry, and rhythmic excitement, both patrons and musicians alike were able to appreciate the composer's efforts and audiences responded with standing ovations. Consequently, new music returned to the regular subscription concerts with sold-out houses. I feel the turning point for the San Francisco Symphony came when John Adams assumed the position of Composer-in-Residence. Along with this change came the earth-shaking decision to repeat new contemporary works instead of presenting them only one time as world premieres. Adams' compositions were programmed again and again, allowing the orchestra and audiences to applaud their complexities. Contemporary music had finally found its own voice within the mainstream of classical music.

The onslaught of *avant-garde* music brought a stream of controversy to the world of classical music and although the 20th Century did produce many great contemporary composers (Igor Stravinsky, Pierre Boulez, John Adams, Béla Bartók, and Arnold Schönberg, to name a few), it seemed audiences still could not get enough of what they considered to be the greatest music ever written (Mozart, Beethoven, Brahms, Wagner, Strauss, *et al.*). As for patrons, many of whom had a difficult time appreciating the great contemporary composers of the 20th Century, to ask them to digest *avant-garde* music seemed beyond their sensibilities. New generations of symphony ticket holders fill today's concert halls and bring with them a more tolerant attitude towards new music. The era of

Cruel and Unmusical compositions has passed and newer and more musical scores with more artistry, passion, and less heartache are finally finding their way into the mainstream of classical music, allowing orchestras to perform a greater amount of music from our own era.

THE BELOVED POPS

Don't play what's there, play what's not there.

—Miles Davis

Although Pops concerts can take place at any time within a symphony season, many are held during summer festivals. Some orchestra contracts offer the Pops as option weeks and, if the truth be told, not all musicians consider them beloved—choosing not to play them at all. Since the bulk of its programming consists of marches, transcriptions of popular tunes, Broadway Theater, movie sound tracks, and a few light classics, it doesn't fall into the most-respected category of music for many classical musicians (even though the stress level is much lower than that of the regular subscription series).

A Pops concert only necessitates one or two rehearsals instead of the usual four (or more) required for the standard season. As a result, a conductor barely has enough time to run through arrangements and practice a few tempo changes. Fortunately, professional musicians do not have trouble sight-reading this music—therefore, very little preparation is required. One exception (an audience favorite) is the *Bolero* by Maurice Ravel which does have very difficult first-chair solos.

The highlight of the Pops and a big draw for audiences are its famous guest soloists. During the years I played with the San Francisco Symphony Pops, it was my privilege to work with such great artists as Victor Borge, Johnny Mathis, Ella Fitzgerald, Tony Bennett, Mel Tormé, Louie Bellson, Pearl Bailey, Rosemary Clooney, George Shearing, Lena Horne, Ray Charles, Andy Williams, Eartha Kitt, The Four Tops, Henry Mancini, and on and on. Most of these soloists do not rehearse—they just show up for the performance. Consequently, the conductor talks musicians through the artist's repertoire and might only get a chance to run through the beginning and ending of a chart. Many of these famous soloists travel with a trio or quartet who have played the same show hundreds of times. They perform alongside the orchestra.

The most successful Pops concerts were conducted by Arthur Fiedler, Director of the Boston Symphony Pops Orchestra from 1930 to 1980. He commissioned Richard Hayman to arrange music of famous pop artists and movie scores for his performances which made his programming unique. Some outstanding favorites came from the Beetles and the popular movie sound tracks of John Williams. The San Francisco Symphony was fortunate to have engaged Fiedler to direct their Pops series for three weeks every summer from 1949 to 1974. He opened each performance with light classical favorites, followed by an intermission, a concerto (usually performed by a young local artist), another intermission, and ended with arrangements of popular songs. The final work on every Fiedler concert was the famous John Philip Sousa March, *Stars and Stripes Forever*.

All Pops concerts were held in Civic Auditorium since this venue could accommodate large audiences of up to six thousand people. The entire ground floor was converted to picnic-style dining for the evening's festivities with potted trees and balloons that surrounded the auditorium and stage, creating an outdoor summer atmosphere. Checkered cloths covered tables, and food and beverages (including alcohol) was served by waiters throughout the evening. Although some people brought their own food, all sorts of vendors were available in the lobby with a large selection of items for purchase. Virtually every performance was sold out.

One Pops concert featured three trumpets in the Leroy Anderson favorite, *Bugler's Holiday*. Two of the players had full beards, but when they stood up to perform the solo, the third trumpet player put on a fake beard, causing orchestra members and Maestro Fiedler to howl with laughter. The audience, not realizing what had happened, laughed along with everyone else.

Another famous Leroy Anderson work is *The Typewriter*. During this piece, a percussionist types on a manual typewriter (the only kind made when it was written) and flips the carriage return in rhythm to the music. Fiedler featured the percussionist as a soloist and had him stand next to the podium, facing the audience. Inevitably, the keys on these old machines got stuck and had to be pulled apart by the player during the performance in order to continue the solo. Near the end of the work, the typewriter rhythms became so fast that the keys jammed and the performer was not able to finish the final measures. To the obvious delight of the audience and in the true spirit of the Pops, he shoved the typewriter off the table. It fell to the floor just as the music ended, creating a spectacular, unrehearsed finale. Fiedler thought it was hilarious and so did everyone else. The Pops concerts were extremely light-hearted and a good time was had by all.

One of Fiedler's favorites was the *Champagne Polka* by Johann Strauss. I was assigned the popgun part (an old vaudeville instrument made from a round tube with a plunger and a cork, tightly fitted into the top). When the plunger is pushed into the tube, air is compressed, forcing the cork out the other end, producing a popping sound. Of course, it is the high point of the work. During the rehearsal, in the exuberance of the moment, I made a very dramatic upward motion, pushing the plunger into the tube, but it only made a soft pop. Fiedler wanted to be sure the popgun would work properly for the performance so the percussionists convened to figure out what had gone wrong. In the end, it was a trumpet colleague (an expert on things mechanical) who came to our rescue. He said there was too much air in the tube, reasoning that when a champagne cork is released, the bottle has only a few inches of air in it even though it makes a very loud pop. He suggested we reduce the air in the tube by starting the plunger nearer the top. It worked and Fiedler was delighted.

When Arthur Fiedler retired, the San Francisco Symphony tried to find a replacement for him by hiring a variety of conductors to lead the orchestra over a period of several years. In the end, however, no one was able to fill the Maestro's shoes or sell out the house as he did. Audiences had fallen in love with this crotchety, old, lovable man with the big white mustache. He knew how to finesse audiences with a well-placed smile while, conversely, giving the orchestra a dirty look (to the delight of patrons) when things did not go as planned, but in the spirit of the Pops, we put up with his antics.

Richard Hayman (Fiedler's arranger) was one of the guest conductors during the search period. He brought some of his own arrangements with him, including his version of John Philip Sousa's *Stars and Stripes Forever*. As mentioned before, Fiedler always ended his programs with Sousa's original score (which did not include timpani). Hayman also did not include timpani when he wrote his arrangement, and since I was the timpanist on the program, when it came time to perform his rendition, I had nothing to play. I always wondered why Sousa did not write for timpani when composing marches since he included them in other orchestral works. So, I called Keith Brion, a Sousa expert and free-lance conductor who directs his own New Sousa Band. This is what he had to say:

Sousa never wrote timpani parts for his marches for several reasons. I think the most likely one is that the resonance of the timpani overtones, which project too strongly through the rather open middle registers of his scoring, obscure the clarity he was seeking. Edwin Franco Goldman described Sousa's preference for tonal balance as being "like an hourglass;" in other words, heavier on the top and bottom but lighter in the mid range. This allowed the all-important upbeats to poke through the texture and create an uplifting, "dancing" feeling to his music. A contemporary quote said that: "Sousa's marches could make a man with a wooden leg stand up and dance." This sort of balance also offered a nice open place for Sousa's elegant counterpoints to be heard.

The percussion section of Sousa's Band was fixed at three players. One played snare drum, one bass drum with cymbal attached, and a third player who played everything else . . . primarily orchestra bell parts, xylophone solos, doubling snare drum passages and, occasionally, timpani for classical transcriptions in some of Sousa's concert music. I know of no instance in which Sousa composed a timpani part for one of his standard marches.

As Sousa's copyrights expired, however, from the 1950s to the present, arrangers and publishers have often added timpani parts to the marches, thinking this would be a way for them to gain fresh copyrights for what had already become public domain music. Some of these arrangements even proclaim to have been the "way Sousa performed it." This is absolutely not true.

I didn't want to sit onstage and not participate in the final piece so I decided to help the percussion section by playing the bass drum (allowing the percussionist to double the snare drum part). As the concert neared the end, I noticed the bass drum part was missing from my music folder and even though I could have played it in its original form from memory, I wanted to be true to Hayman's arrangement since he was conducting. So, catching the eye of the Principal Librarian, John Van Winkle, who was standing in the wings, I motioned to him that the part was missing from my folder. He gave me a "high" sign and went backstage to look for it. During the penultimate work on the program, right before *Stars and Stripes Forever,* he returned, waving the part at me from offstage. While the audience applauded, I ran, grabbed the music and placed it on my stand. When I opened the folder, all I saw was a blank piece of music paper with three words written in large black letters: BOOM, BOOM, BOOM! When I turned to look at John, he was laughing hysterically. Consequently, I did have to fake it but, fortunately, Hayman was not aware of any missing booms. I still have this famous bass drum arrangement in my files and it will remain there for perpetuity. The Pops concerts were a fun-filled experience, enjoyed by musicians, soloists, conductors, audiences, and even librarians.

Another San Francisco Symphony tradition, *A Night in Old Vienna,* takes place every New Year's Eve and is, for all purposes, a Pops concert of Viennese favorites. The orchestra performs from

9:00 p.m. to 11:00 p.m., when a Big Band takes over with onstage dancing until the wee hours of the morning.

During my first season with the Symphony, I was assigned the shotgun part to Johann Strauss' *Hunting Polka*. I believe it was more a rite of initiation than anything else. This part requires a pistol (loaded with blanks) to be shot at a precise moment in the music. During a Pops concert, however, nothing is ever that simple. While wearing the standard evening attire (black tux), I also had to don a medieval hunting hat and carry a shotgun while roaming around the stage, looking skyward for prey—in other words, I was now an actor! Then, on cue, I pulled the trigger as a crew member (hovering out of sight in the rafters) dropped a dead turkey in front of me (de-feathered and ready for the pot). If that wasn't embarrassing enough, I had to pick the bird up by the neck, walk to the podium, and present it to Maestro Josef Krips who just stood there with a big grin on his face as the rest of the orchestra laughed. Finally, I took a bow and sheepishly walked back to my place in the percussion section, dragging the turkey behind me.

Some symphony orchestras have moved away from a Pops identification, creating different monikers, such as, *Summer in the City* or *Summer and the Symphony*. Many of these music festivals feature only one composer, for example, the popular *Mostly Mozart*

series. The San Francisco Symphony also performs *Beethoven,* *Mahler, Baroque, Schubert-Berg, Russian,* and *Maverick Festivals.*

In my opinion, nothing will ever replace Arthur Fiedler and the San Francisco Symphony Pops. And although it may have lacked some artistry and passion, the atmosphere he created, featuring casual dining during performances, famous pop artists, light classical music, and a laid-back, capricious attitude on the podium generated a charismatic aura of high-spirited fun and superb entertainment. I haven't polled the orchestra but I'm sure they would agree two intermissions during a concert instead of the usual one is very appealing. There is no doubt that Arthur Fiedler and the San Francisco Symphony Pops were highly *Beloved* in Bay Area music circles.

ETHICS IN THE WORKPLACE

If a literary man puts together two words about music, one of them will be wrong.

—Aaron Copland

When considering the topic of ethics in the workplace, honesty has to be on the top of the list. Today, some CEOs "cook the books" to hide losses, pay exorbitant bonuses to executives even though a company is losing money, and devise "Ponzi" schemes to deceive investors. American orchestras are non-profit corporations with the majority of their operating revenue derived from donations, ticket sales, and an endowment fund. Musicians do not monitor, control, or influence an orchestra's finances. Nevertheless, they still have a certain level of honesty to maintain as performers.

Highly-trained professional players give more than one hundred percent effort during rehearsals and concerts. When it comes to rhythmic accuracy, impeccable intonation, tremendously loud dynamics, or an almost inaudible whisper, musicians model the concept of work ethics. Honesty, however, can become an issue if a player does not adhere to these principles.

When I first joined the orchestra, I was told about a violinist who gave the impression of playing with virtuosity even though his bow did not always touch the strings! The fact that each section string player performs the same part makes it possible for one musician to be dishonest by not executing all of the written notes. This is not feasible in the brass, woodwind, and percussion sections since only one player is assigned to a part.

The characteristics of commitment, consistency, and camaraderie are all necessary ethical elements in any profession, but even more so in a large symphony orchestra. Members depend on colleagues in order to make accurate entrances or to maintain consistent dynamic control, assuring the entire orchestra sounds as one voice. Individualism, consequently, is not a desired characteristic in this profession inasmuch as all musicians must work together as team players.

Young string players, new to orchestral life, experience a time of adjustment as they learn this concept of working together, considering much of their training has been performing concertos (where the solo line projects above the ensemble). The exact opposite is true for members of an orchestra since they are required to play only one part of the entire musical score. Likewise, as each musician must balance with other players in a section, all sections of an orchestra have their own level of exposure (within the composition) and cannot rise above or fall below that determined dynamic. Musicians also need to be constantly aware of the conductor who can interject a minor adjustment into the music with the slightest gesture of the baton, a facial expression, or the hands.

There is no better way to learn how to become a team player than by performing in an orchestra or smaller ensemble (string quartet, piano trio, brass and woodwind choir, band, or percussion ensemble). The idea of "sticking out" in this profession is not only distracting but irritating, and whether it comes from incorrect bowing, an unpleasant attitude, or joking around, it doesn't take much to annoy other musicians and interfere with the team-player concept.

Many years ago, a new member joined the orchestra who had the reputation of being a virtuoso violinist. During rehearsal intermissions, he played excerpts from the famous Paganini Caprice etudes (backstage) demonstrating exquisite technique (to the astonishment of other string players). While onstage, however, he was unhappy because he had to perform within a section where his sound blended with sixty other musicians. He resigned after a few years.

Another violinist, who sat in the back of the section, regularly left the stage during rehearsals (with a book in his back pocket) and returned about fifteen minutes later. He didn't seem to care what others thought and showed little camaraderie or personal integrity to fellow colleagues by leaving in the middle of a session. At least that was the impression he gave orchestra members. But, it is also possible his absences were due to pain. Before carpal-tunnel syndrome and arthritic-joint problems became accepted topics of discussion, players rarely complained about the physical suffering they endured while performing for fear of criticism, demotion, or termination of employment. Some musicians, therefore, performed in constant discomfort, never mentioning their agony to anyone. This could have been the case with this individual. It's possible he was trying to alleviate pain by resting whenever it became too intense. It's different today—musicians who suffer from debilitating injuries because of continuous, repetitive motions, not only seek medical help, but may have to take sick leave of up to one year.

Empathy is a good quality to have as performers since everyone is prone to making mistakes. Whether losing one's place in the music, playing an incorrect dynamic or phrasing, missing an entrance, fingering or striking a wrong note, occasional poor intonation, or shaky rhythm, musicians can be their own worst critics. A conductor or even a colleague can look at a player in a disapproving manner when a mistake is made (which is totally out of place since most players never repeat the same error). During such times, empathy is a more appropriate attitude.

Richard Osborne quotes a trombonist with the London Philharmonia Orchestra regarding a rehearsal of Richard Strauss' *Don Juan* in his book, *Herbert von Karajan: A Life in Music* (Excerpt by Richard Osborne from *Herbert Von Karajan: A Life in Music*" [© Richard Osborne, 1998] is reproduced by permission of PFD (www.PFD.co.uk) on behalf of Richard Osborne):

> *I've always respected von Karajan, simply because he treated you man to man. The first time I played with him we were doing Don Juan. I was a new face in the orchestra, very inexperienced, I'd never played the piece, though I'd studied it and practiced my part. Well, in the beginning the strings sweep up, and then*

there are the basses and the bass trombone, which has the phrase on the beat, and it has to be there. Von Karajan made some loose, ethereal movement which the strings understood and the first fiddle led them up the sweep. But, I couldn't feel or see a downbeat at all—he just had his arms in the air, he wasn't going to beat like a bandmaster—and I missed the entry. I think most conductors would have stopped and made a song and dance. Von Karajan looked over, as if to say, "I know my job, I hope you know yours. I won't say anything and we'll see what you do." When the recapitulation came, of course, I was ready and played it. He just glanced over again, as if to say OK, but not a word was spoken. Von Karajan was fine. Well, he was a real man, a real musician. I could get on with a man like that.

Criticism can also become an ethical issue. As professional musicians, we accept criticism regarding musical concepts from conductors but, at times, it can approach harassment. Some conductors seem to have a "thing" about stopping a rehearsal to correct obvious mistakes which is a waste of time and does not bode well with members of an orchestra. Rather, conductors should spend valuable rehearsal time working on musical elements (dynamics, phrasing, rhythmic precision, and intonation) that would result in a more impassioned performance.

When a music director is displeased with a musician's performance, the player can be called into the maestro's office for a meeting. This often places the orchestra member in a disadvantaged position because it is difficult to respond to one-sided criticism. One person's opinion, especially that of a conductor, is difficult to challenge. What can one say in response to a conductor's displeasure with regard to a player's sound, rhythm, or intonation? Performers, whenever possible, always try to adjust to constructive suggestions but, depending on the tone of the meeting, such a conference can damage a musician's sense of security and affect his or her performance. The players' committee, therefore, suggests that if a member of the orchestra is called into a meeting by the music director, the chair (or another committee member) be present to witness the conversation in case further action is taken against the player.

Generally, musicians develop a brick wall to reflect negative criticism. The fact is, as soon as performers step onstage, in front of an audience, they are subject to criticism. Contrary musical opinions are part of the music business and as members of an orchestra, players soon learn that professional critics are in the business of entertaining the public—thus, their comments are taken with a "grain of salt." When reading concert reviews, musicians often disagree with a critic's analysis. Whether it has to do with comments regarding tempo, dynamics, balance, or an individual player's contribution, many performers find it hard to believe they heard the same program as the critic who reviewed the show. Although there are well-respected music critics, some deserve the old adage: "If you can't play, you teach, and if you can't teach, you become a music critic!"

George Bernard Shaw, celebrated Irish-born playwright and critic, quotes Dr. Villiers Stanford's (Irish-born composer) view on the subject of criticism. Shaw also mentions that it was the best article he had ever read on this subject. It is taken from Eric Bentley's *Shaw on Music* (Doubleday Anchor Book, NY):

> *I say, as one who is, from much experience in the musician's craft, perhaps exceptionally quick in seizing the points of a new work at first hearing, that to expect the best possible criticism, or indeed criticism of any lasting value at all under such circumstances is grotesque; and the insistence upon such hot haste production is a hardship to the writer, an injury to the producer, and a mischief to the public.*

As much as Shaw was impressed by the quote, he added:

> *I am not sure that the opinion elaborated in a week is always so much more valuable than the impression made in a moment.*

He further opines regarding music from the Classical Period which has been in the repertoire for hundreds of years:

> *The only musical compositions which will bear thinking of for more than half an hour are those which require an intimate acquaintance of at least ten years for their critical mastery.*

The San Francisco Symphony performs summer concerts at Stern Grove, a beautiful outdoor park in the City where most listeners bring a blanket and picnic lunch and sit on the expansive grassy area to enjoy the program. Many concert goers show up at 10:00 a.m. for the rehearsal and stay through the performance that ends at 4:00 p.m. (even though most of the day is shrouded in heavy fog). One particular concert featured ballet music and as it happened (most likely due to an injury to one of the dancers), the program was changed at the last minute—however, the critic's review included the cancelled work. In other words, he either did not attend the concert or left early and concocted a review for the newspaper. So much for ethics in journalism!

Other ethical concerns revolve around age discrimination. Music directors not only conduct the majority of concerts during an orchestra's season, but are also in charge of all musical decisions regarding orchestra personnel. The relationship between a music director and an individual player can be tricky business. Musicians who were hired by the current director, most likely, become part of the "inner circle" and feel confident in their positions; however, orchestra members brought in by previous directors can feel less secure because every conductor has different demands, baton techniques, and expectations that emerge once they assume the podium. And, yes, age discrimination does exist in a symphony orchestra. A rumor once spread around the San Francisco Symphony that one particular music director hired twenty-year-old female performers with thirty years of experience!

Erich Leinsdorf talks about the time he was engaged to perform Mahler's Symphony No. 4 with the Houston Symphony (1970s) with only four rehearsals. He told management it made no sense for them to pretend they could learn and prepare such difficult music in the same amount of time it took the New York Philharmonic or the Chicago Symphony. The following quote is from his book, *Cadenza: A Musical Career* (Houghton Mifflin Company, Boston):

> *It was alarming to me, because one of the basic tenets in any of the performing arts is that young and less experienced talent should grow with the years to maturity and mastery. It looked to me as if the concept of equality had been misunderstood and misapplied. On graduation day we have perhaps talent, aptitude, drive, ambition, and skill. After that come the years when we acquire the subtler qualities a musician must possess to be an artist.*

Alan Jefferson also champions age and experience in *An Anatomy of the Orchestra* (Crane, Russak & Company, NY):

> *Playing in an orchestra requires a special kind of technique which comes only from experience in doing it. Nor does this technique, once gained, stop there. I know a clarinetist who says he still learns new ways of playing; of covering up mistakes, defects or slips by himself and others; of getting around difficult passages in new ways—all this after twenty years in the same seat. This is indeed progression, for this admirable man knows he will never be an acknowledged soloist, yet continues to perfect his art within the framework in which he works. It is the player who,*

after five years, thinks he knows it all and lets up for a
moment, who finds himself in appalling trouble.

One way orchestra musicians have countered age discrimination is by negotiating seniority pay into the contract. This incentive rewards experienced players for long-time service. On the flip side, music directors can still make changes by reseating older musicians. This, of course, causes anxiety, not only for those being reseated, but among orchestra members in general who wonder about their own status. Some demotions are made to provide open chairs near the front of a section for new, younger, impressionable hires. But, as previously mentioned, although it may be true that older players lose some dexterity, it is easily compensated for by their years of performing experience. Regarding non-renewal (termination of a player's contract), language is on the side of the musician because it's very difficult to prove material failure to perform at the artistic level of the orchestra.

David Schneider, former Principal Second Violin of the San Francisco Symphony, addressed the subject of age discrimination in his book, *The San Francisco Symphony* (Presidio Press, Novato, CA):

> *Ironically, youth had been glorified in the orchestra from the time* [Seiji] *Ozawa took over. At one time to be young was to be inexperienced, and maestros were wary of inexperience. But from the time of Ozawa's ascension to the San Francisco Symphony podium, the clarion call was "Get them here young and hot—I'll teach them what they have to know about orchestra playing." I cannot dispute the fact that young musicians now entering the orchestra are,*

on the average, better instrumental technicians than in previous years. But other qualities are necessary for good orchestral playing—flexibility, awareness of nuances, and a feel for the piece in one's bones, sinews, heart, and mind that comes only from playing works hundreds of times—in other words, experience.

All members of an orchestra, except the concertmaster, have tenure, giving them confidence they cannot be randomly dismissed by the "Boss" without due process. Tenure, however, is a two-edged sword. On one hand, it protects musicians from unscrupulous music directors who could arbitrarily dismiss them; on the other hand, it defends those who may not fully contribute their talents to such a demanding profession.

Music directors want to bring in as many new players as possible during their time with an orchestra. By selecting new members with a particular sound or style, they hope to create their personal concept of a *world-class* orchestra. As musicians, we have often heard this term used by conductors but what some fail to realize is that reaching world-class status requires two primary conditions:

1. *Salary and Benefits:* This is usually not a problem for management because they understand an orchestra can only attract the best players if its salary and benefits

are comparable to (what used to be) the "Big Five" orchestras (New York Philharmonic, Boston Symphony, Philadelphia Orchestra, Chicago Symphony, and Cleveland Orchestra). Today, it is more likely to be the "Big Ten" or "Fifteen."

2. *A Music Director's Musical Ability:* Another important factor an orchestra must consider if it hopes to reach this elusive goal of world-class prominence is for the board of directors to hire a music director who has the ability to inspire musicians to perform as a world-class orchestra.

In my opinion, such a music director should possess:

- A clear beating pattern
- The ability to maintain a steady pulse (does not rush)
- The talent to create a musical phrase and to be able to communicate it to players
- A charismatic presence on the podium
- A significant knowledge of an instrument's technical capacity
- Common sense that supports musicians instead of humiliating them
- A social presence with the board of directors and patrons of the arts for fund raising
- A large repertoire of Classical, Romantic and, most importantly, Contemporary music

- An inspiring rehearsal technique
- A reasonable command of the English language
- The ability to memorize large scores
- An impeccable sense of intonation
- A flawless sense of rhythm
- The expertise to select outstanding musicians from auditions
- A vision for an orchestra's future: the selection of out-standing soloists, guest conductors, chamber music, children's concerts, new-music series, run-out concerts within the local community, touring, recordings, television series, fund raising, music festivals, summer series, and a youth orchestra

The music director, management, and the board of directors have as much (or more) to do with a symphony orchestra attaining world-class status as do the musicians.

It is also fair to expect ethical behavior from an audience. Two highly unusual occurrences took place during the Viet Nam War era. The first one happened immediately after the orchestra finished playing the *National Anthem* (a San Francisco Symphony tradition at the opening performance of every season). When the *Star Spangled Banner* concluded, a man from the audience yelled out: "Not in this War!" And, although Josef Krips, the conductor, was temporarily stunned, he quickly recovered to begin the concert.

Another anti-war statement took place during a performance of the *National Anthem*. This time, as soon as the orchestra began to play, a man seated in the first tier of box seats climbed over the railing and, holding on with both hands, "mooned" the conductor and orchestra. Fortunately, he kept his pants on and was quickly escorted out of the hall by security guards.

The majority of musicians (with very few exceptions) hold to an amazingly high standard of excellence because of their musical training, discipline, perseverance, and work ethics, honed since early childhood. Rehearsals and concerts are considered a challenge for professional musicians and they strive to perform with perfection in search of pure artistry. In fact, musicians have such high work ethics, they are their own worst critics, and no matter how well they perform, players constantly aim to further excel at this demanding craft. That's just how it is. Unless musicians are performing with pain, their passion is to give one hundred percent effort. The thought of holding back, taking it easy, sloppy playing, mediocre intonation, not paying attention, slipshod rhythms, weak dynamics, or careless phrasing, seldom happens. The concentration required to perform a two-hour rehearsal or concert is extreme, especially for the strings who rarely have long periods of rests.

Thousands of notes are performed in any given composition, each one requiring precise hand positions, fingering, and/ or correct embouchure in order to articulate the proper character, dynamic, and phrasing. The brain has to be several measures ahead of the eyes in order to anticipate the necessary techniques to execute a passage. The eyes must be measures ahead of physical motions to play the notes and rhythms accurately. With tempos such as *allegro, presto,* and *prestissimo* (fast, very fast, and fastest), decisions are made in micro seconds and those who have fewer notes (for example, percussionists, the tuba player, and harpist) have to count rests or listen for musical cues in order to make proper entrances. It doesn't take much to lose one's place in the music if the mind is allowed to wander. When it comes to the subject of work ethics, there is no better example in the workplace than that of a professional musician.

SUCCESS ≠ HAPPINESS

Music is a strange thing. I would almost say it is a miracle.
For it stands halfway between thought and phenomenon,
between spirit and matter.

—Heinrich Heine

No one achieves great success without sacrifice, dedication, perseverance, passion, and heartache. Rising to the top of any profession requires a life-long commitment to excellence and with it comes personal satisfaction, security, and financial reward. Yet, success does not always guarantee happiness. We often hear of businessmen and women, actors, politicians, and artists who make it to the top of a career only to live lives of hopeless desperation, sickness, and/or loneliness. What is it about success that causes some to miss the mark when it comes to their personal lives?

Professional musicians spend an inordinate amount of time practicing in order to maintain technique and learn new music. Besides juggling a major orchestra schedule, many players perform in chamber music ensembles or hold teaching positions in universities and conservatories; others compose, conduct, and participate in a variety of music-related activities. These never-ending endeavors leave little time to master the personal life skills so necessary for enduring friendships and close relationships.

The energy required to excel in music is the same energy needed to excel in life. Heinrich Heine's quote in the header to this chapter says, *Music is a strange thing.* But, can't we say that about all of life? He continues: *For it* [music] *stands halfway between thought and phenomenon, between spirit and matter.* Musicians can easily spend a lot of energy on the "matter" of making music and leave little time for the "spirit" of life. Perhaps happiness also stands halfway between one's career and the spiritual insight necessary to maintain a meaningful balance.

This book was written for patrons of the arts because it is YOU who applaud the majesty, grandeur, artistry, beauty, passion, and excitement of great music. It is YOUR endless support that encourages musicians, conductors, and composers to devote their lives to such a challenging profession. Hopefully, this backstage tour has offered the reader insights into the magnificence of *The Great American Symphony Orchestra.*

APPENDIX A
Instruments as Listed in a Musical Score

WOODWINDS:
   a. Flute (including Piccolo)
   b. Oboe (including English Horn)
   c. Clarinet (including Bass Clarinet)
   d. Bassoon (including Contrabassoon)

BRASS:
   a. French Horn
   b. Trumpet
   c. Trombone
   d. Tuba

PIANO & HARP: Each instrument is its own section

PERCUSSION:
   a. Timpani
   b. Percussion

STRINGS:

a. Violin I

b. Violin II

c. Viola

d. Cello

e. Bass

APPENDIX B
Symphony Administration
& Staff Positions

The Board of Governors: President, Three Vice-Presidents, Corporate Secretary (Non-Musical Contracts), Committee Chairs, including: Artistic Policy, Audit, Education, Youth Orchestra, Nominating, & Development

The Executive Director's Office: Executive Director, Executive Assistant

Artistic Planning: Director of Artistic Planning, Artist Liaison, Chorus Manager, Artistic Planning Assistant, Artistic Administrator, Assistant to the Director of Artistic Planning

Education Programs/Youth Orchestra: Director of Education & Youth Orchestra, Manager of Education Programs, Administrative Assistant, Education Program Assistant, Coordinator of Education Programs, Program Administrator, Community of Music Makers

Development: Executive Assistant, Director for Major Gifts, Development Systems Analyst, Director of Corporate

Gifts, Gift Planning Associate, Manager of Corporate Gifts, Development Research Associate, Campaign Associate, Institutional Gifts Coordinator, Director of Proposal Development, Manager of Annual Giving Societies, Director of Membership Gifts, Membership Gifts Coordinator, Manager of Foundation & Government Relations, Campaign Manager of Donor Stewardship & Events, Senior Major Gifts Officer, Development Coordinator, Individual Gifts Coordinator, Associate Director of Development, Wattis Room Manager, Director of Gift Planning, Major Gifts Coordinator, Director of Annual Gift Societies

Volunteer Council: Director of Special Events & Volunteer Services, Project Manager, Volunteer Council Coordinator, Administrative Assistant

Finance: Chief Financial Officer, Senior Financial Analyst, Senior Accountant, Executive Assistant, Donor Records Analyst, Payroll Manager, Manager of Financial Analysis & Reporting, Controller, Staff Accountant

Information Technology: Chief Information Officer, Executive Assistant, Manager of Staffing & Employer Relations, Manager of Employer Benefits

Human Resources: Director of Human Resources, Executive Assistant, Manager for Staffing & Employee Relations, Manager of Employee Benefits

Marketing, Communications & External Affairs: Director, Executive Assistant

Marketing & Sales: Director of Marketing, Campaign Coordinator, Media Services Assistant, Digital Marketing Coordinator, Media Services Manager, Assistant Media Services Manager, Media Services Coordinator, Campaign Manager, Digital Marketing Assistant, Senior Campaign Manager

Public Relations: Director of Public Relations, Public Relations Manager, Senior Publicist

Publications: Publications Editor & Special Projects, Publications Associate, Associate Archivist, Managing Editor, Archivist, Program Editor

Patron Services: Director, Patron Services Manager, Box Office Manager, Assistant Box Office Manager, Benefactor Ticket Coordinator, Patron Services Representatives

General Manager's Division: General Manager, Executive Assistant

Electronic Media & Tours: Electronic Media Manager, Electronic Media Coordinator, Keeping Score Education Director, Manager of Tours & Media Production

Operations: Director, Production Manager, Telecommunications Coordinator, Operations Manager, Office Service Clerk

Retail: Manager of Retail Operations, Manager of Repeat Performance Shop, Symphony Store Manager

Orchestra Personnel: Orchestra Personnel Manager, Orchestra Personnel Administrator, Assistant Orchestra Personnel Manager

Music Library: Principal Librarian, Two Assistant Librarians

ABOUT THE AUTHOR

 **A**nthony J. Cirone received his Bachelor of Science and Master of Science degrees from The Juilliard School where he studied with Saul Goodman, solo timpanist of the New York Philharmonic. In 1965 upon graduation, he joined the San Francisco Symphony as a percussionist under Music Director, Josef Krips, and served as Professor of Music at San José State University until 2001. While at San José he headed the Percussion Department and also taught courses in Manuscript Preparation and Computer Engraving. Cirone also served on the faculties of San Francisco State University, Stanford University, and was Chairman of the Percussion Department at Indiana University, Bloomington. His students have gone on to hold positions in major orchestras and universities around the world.

A prolific composer, Cirone has over 100 published titles, including textbooks (most recently *Cirone's Pocket Dictionary of Foreign Musical Terms*), 3 symphonies for percussion, 4 sonatas, a string quartet, and 7 works for orchestra. He is the Executive Percussion Consultant/Editor for Meredith Music Publications and the author of *Portraits In Rhythm*, a text for training percussionists that has become a standard worldwide.

Tony received a *Special Distinction Award* from ASCAP, won the Modern Drummer Magazine *Reader's Poll for Classical Percussionist* five years in a row, was inducted into the prestigious Percussive Arts Society *Hall of Fame*, and recently was awarded the Music Publishers Association's Paul Revere Award for Graphic Excellence. As an active clinician, he represents several international companies including, Avedis Zildjian Company, Yamaha Corporation, Remo Inc., and Malletech Corporation. You can visit Anthony J. Cirone on Facebook or contact him at *ajcirone@aol.com*